STRONG WHERE STRENGTH IS NEEDED

When you see ATHOL on a tool you know that it is a warranty of the best.

Athol Machine Co.
INCORPORATED 1868

MANUFACTURERS OF

Athol and Starrett Vises, Machinery, Fine Tools, Hardware Specialties, Castings

ATHOL, MASSACHUSETTS, U. S. A.

Catalogue 34

Cable Address — Choppers, Athol
Codes — Atlantic Cable, Western Union

ATHOL MACHINE COMPANY

THIS WARRANTY STANDS BEHIND EVERY ATHOL AND STARRETT VISE

AND EVERY ATHOL MACHINE AND TOOL.

We warrant all our vises and tools to be free from defects of material or workmanship. Any vise found defective in either particular will be replaced without charge.

When you buy ATHOL and STARRETT PATENT VISES and ATHOL TOOLS AND MACHINERY you buy Service unexcelled. Quality unsurpassed, and the surety that we intend to have every customer satisfied.

WE LEAVE IT TO YOU.
YOU ARE THE JUDGE.

If for some reason you are dissatisfied, write us. We will make good. We believe the GOLDEN RULE can be followed even where vise predominates. Give us a chance to add you to our list of friends and customers.

We are not afraid to endorse our warranty with our signature.

Athol Machine Co.
By *[signature]*
Gen'l Manager and Supt.

STRONG WHERE STRENGTH IS NEEDED

ATHOL VISES AND TOOLS, ATHOL, MASS., U. S. A.

PLEASE NOTE

Our goods are made by skilled mechanics and are carefully inspected. We agree to replace anything found to be defective in material or construction.

For special warranty in regard to Vises, see page 2.

When goods are returned for repairs or for other reason, the name of the sender must be plainly marked on the package, and the transportation charges prepaid. A letter giving full information as to what is wanted should be mailed at the time goods are sent.

Mechanics and manufacturers are requested to order our goods through hardware dealers. In places in the United States and Canada where the trade do not sell our goods, we will send them prepaid on receipt of prices given in this Catalogue.

Dealers without adequate commerical rating, desiring credit, must furnish satisfactory references.

Goods will not be sent C. O. D. unless the order is accompanied by a sufficient amount to pay transportation charges both ways.

Our goods are sold to dealers f. o. b. here, at purchaser's risk after shipment.

Customers are requested to give specific shipping directions with each order. In the absence of such instruction we shall ship, at purchaser's risk, by what we consider the best way, safety, quickness and cheapness being considered.

If desired, we can join our shipments with goods being sent by **The L. S. Starrett Co.** of this place.

This edition, No. 34, includes all the items shown in our Vise and Machinery Catalogue No. 32 and our Tool Catalogue No. 33.

Order by number, to save time and mistakes.

TO SELL VISES

Don't Keep Them in a Corner Down Cellar; Put Them Where People Will See Them

The illustrations on the following pages show stands we are supplying the trade for the display of our vises. **These stands are not sold but loaned.** They remain the property of the Athol Machine Co. and are to be used only for displaying Athol Machine Co. vises. They are sent only in connection with an order for vises as per lists, or equivalent in value.

Any other of our vises having the same width of jaw may be substituted for the numbers given in schedule, the list and net price, of course, changing according to the vises selected. In case we do not have a certain size of vise in stock we will substitute in order to avoid delay in shipment. This will make a slight variation in price.

ELECTROTYPES

We shall be glad to furnish electrotypes of our goods, as per illustrations herein, free to any dealer who may care to use them.

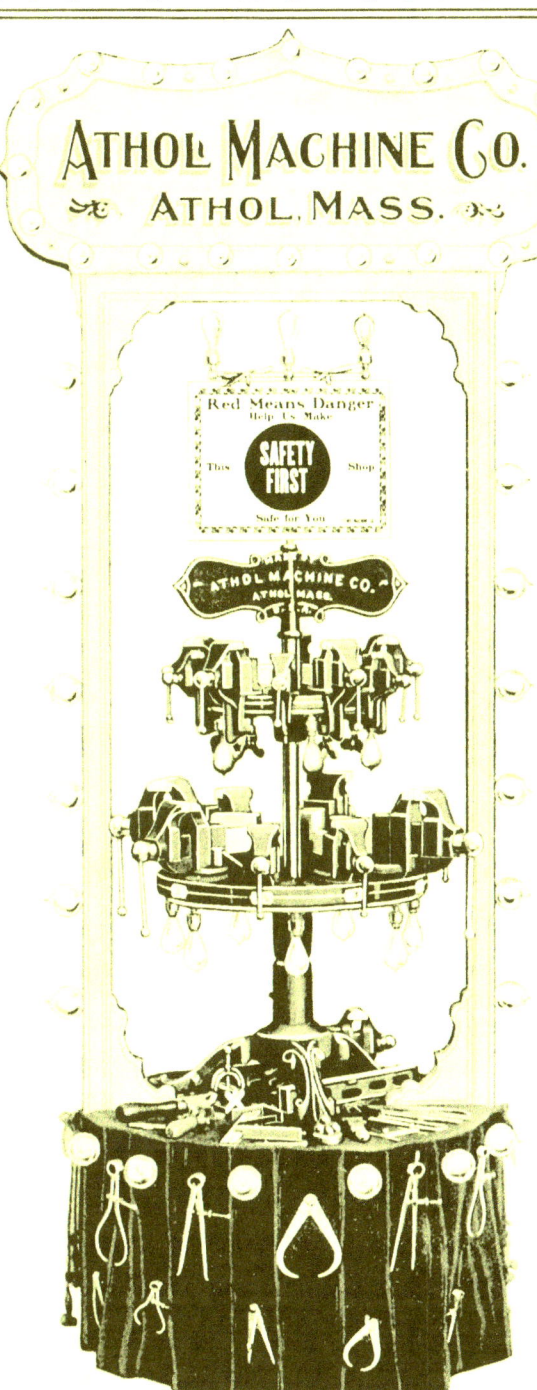

ELECTRIC DISPLAY STAND

Revolving Display Stand used to show the Athol Machine Co.'s products at Conventions and Expositions. It has also been used for window displays.

The Display Stand has both alternating and direct current motors, carries nearly 100 lights and makes a very attractive appearance.

ATHOL MACHINE COMPANY

A

VISE DISPLAY STAND
No. A

With Two Shelves for Counter Display of
Starrett Improved Patented Vises

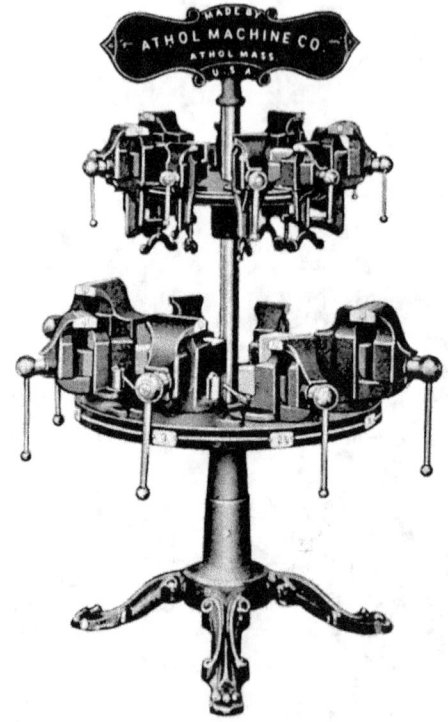

Height, 39 in.; extreme dia. with Vises, 30 in.

For Domestic Shipment
Weight of Stand, crated, 100 lbs.
Total weight of shipment, including Vises, 362 lbs.

For Ocean Shipment
Weight of Stand, boxed, net 68 lbs., gross 116 lbs.
Total weight of shipment, including Vises, net 306 lbs., gross 380 lbs.
Total measurement of 2 cases, 8.06 cu. ft.
Every Vise fully warranted—See Page 2. Write us for prices and information.

ATHOL VISES AND TOOLS, ATHOL, MASS., U.S.A.

ATHOL VISES

List of Starrett Improved Patented Vises Sent with Vise Display Stand No. A

No. Vises	Weight Each	Total Weight	List Each	Total List
5—701	2¾ lbs.	13¾ lbs.	$2.50	$12.50
5—703	6 lbs.	30 lbs.	3.50	17.50
4—704	7½ lbs.	30 lbs.	5.75	23.00
2—705	6 lbs.	12 lbs.	4.75	9.50
2—706	11½ lbs.	23 lbs.	6.50	13.00
1—724	18 lbs.	18 lbs.	8.50	8.50
2—707	10 lbs.	20 lbs.	5.25	10.50
3—708	19 lbs.	57 lbs.	7.50	22.50
2—709	16½ lbs.	33 lbs.	6.00	12.00
26		236¾		$129.00

The Starrett Improved Patented Vises, as listed above, offer the Dealer a chance to keep continually in front of his Customers the easiest selling Vise ever placed on the market and the one most productive in repeat orders—where his real profit lies.

The Starrett Improved Patented Vises have a handle that stays where it is put, that can be moved instantly to any desired position without moving the jaws, that can be brought where the workman can get a lift on it to tighten the work in the vise, and that is never in the way.

The corrugated base and bolt head gives the swivel base Vise a positive lock in any position. No pins to stick; no friction clamp to slip; can be locked in any position the full diameter of the circle.

No mechanic can see one of these Vises without wanting it.

B ## VISE DISPLAY STAND
No. B

With Three Shelves for Floor Display of Starrett Improved Patented Vises

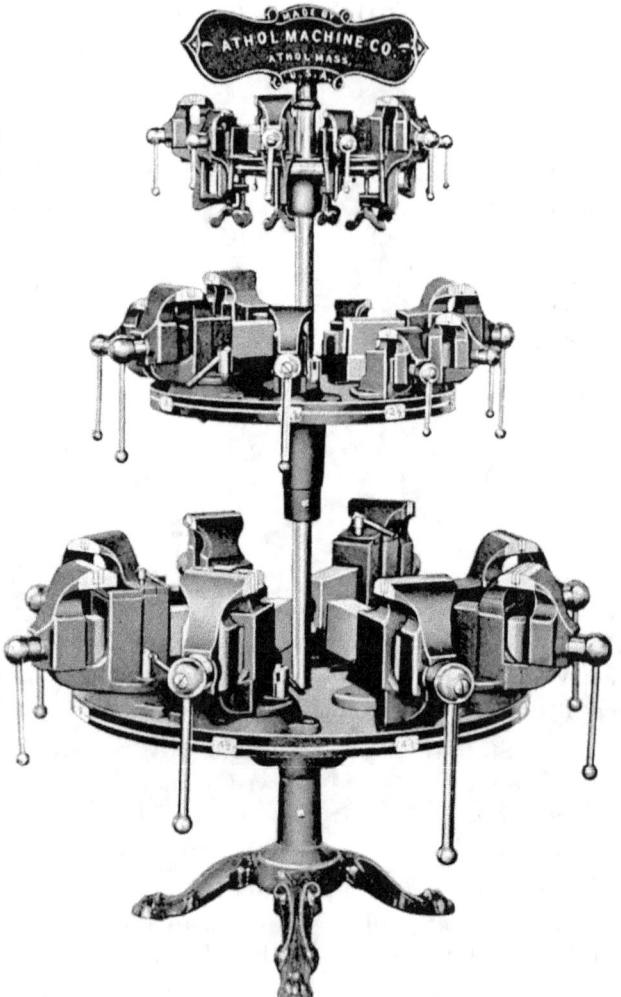

Height, 57 in.; extreme dia., with Vises, 45 in.

For Domestic Shipment

Weight of Stand, crated, 143 lbs. Total weight of shipment, including Vises, 650 lbs.

For Ocean Shipment

Weight of Stand, boxed, net 125 lbs., gross 190 lbs.

Total weight of shipment, including Vises, net 607 lbs., gross 725 lbs.

Total measurement of 3 cases, 17 cu. ft.

Every Vise fully warranted—See Page 2. Write us for prices and full information.

ATHOL VISES

List of Starrett Improved Patented Vises Sent with Vise Display Stand No. B

No. Vises	Weight Each	Total Weight	List Each	Total List
5 701	2¾ lbs.	13¾ lbs.	$2.50	$12.50
5 703	6 lbs.	30 lbs.	3.50	17.50
2 704	7½ lbs.	15 lbs.	5.75	11.50
1 705	6 lbs.	6 lbs.	4.75	4.75
1 706	11½ lbs.	11½ lbs.	6.50	6.50
1 707	10 lbs.	10 lbs.	5.25	5.25
1 708	19 lbs.	19 lbs.	7.50	7.50
1 709	16½ lbs.	16½ lbs.	6.00	6.00
1 724	18 lbs.	18 lbs.	8.50	8.50
2 710	31 lbs.	62 lbs.	8.75	17.50
1 730	49 lbs.	49 lbs.	13.25	13.25
1 711	27 lbs.	27 lbs.	7.00	7.00
2 712	49 lbs.	98 lbs.	10.50	21.00
1 713	40 lbs.	40 lbs.	8.50	8.50
1 714	66 lbs.	66 lbs.	12.50	12.50
26		481¾		$159.75

Mr. Dealer: — Did you ever stop to think of the difference it must make in your sales of Vises if they are kept on one of our Vise Display Stands, where your customers can see them, or if they are kept in some dark cellar or under a counter?

The Display Stand saves the time of your salesmen in pulling vises out for inspection and putting them back again, and prevents the chance of the particular vise the customer desires escaping notice entirely. In addition the space occupied by these stands is much less than would be needed by any other method of displaying vises.

Bring your Vises out in the sunlight and see what a difference it makes in your sales.

ATHOL MACHINE COMPANY

C VISE DISPLAY STAND
No. C

With Two Shelves for Counter Display of Standard, Six Hundred Line and Simpson Vises

Height, 39 in.; extreme dia. with Vises, 30 in.

For Domestic Shipment

Weight of Stand, crated, 100 lbs. Total weight of shipment, including Vises, 540 lbs.

For Ocean Shipment

Weight of Stand, boxed, net 68 lbs., gross 116 lbs.
Total weight of shipment, including Vises, net 485 lbs., gross 580 lbs.
Total measurement of 3 cases, 11.27 cu. ft.
Every Vise fully warranted—See Page 2. Prices and full information given upon request.

ATHOL VISES AND TOOLS, ATHOL, MASS., U. S. A.

ATHOL VISES

LIST OF SIMPSON, STANDARD AND SIX HUNDRED LINE VISES SENT WITH VISE DISPLAY STAND No. C.

No. Vises	Weight Each	Total Weight	List Each	Total List
3 0	$1\frac{1}{2}$ lbs.	$4\frac{1}{2}$ lbs.	$1.25	$3.75
2 1	$2\frac{3}{4}$ lbs.	$5\frac{1}{2}$ lbs.	1.75	3.50
3 2	$5\frac{3}{4}$ lbs.	$17\frac{1}{4}$ lbs.	2.75	8.25
2 3	$1\frac{1}{2}$ lbs.	3 lbs.	1.40	2.80
2 4	$2\frac{3}{4}$ lbs.	$5\frac{1}{2}$ lbs.	2.00	4.00
1 5	$5\frac{3}{4}$ lbs.	$5\frac{3}{4}$ lbs.	3.15	3.15
1 10	$6\frac{1}{4}$ lbs.	$6\frac{1}{4}$ lbs.	5.75	5.75
1 11	$9\frac{1}{2}$ lbs.	$9\frac{1}{2}$ lbs.	6.50	6.50
1 27	$5\frac{1}{2}$ lbs.	$5\frac{1}{2}$ lbs.	4.75	4.75
1 29	$15\frac{1}{2}$ lbs.	$15\frac{1}{2}$ lbs.	6.00	6.00
1 145	43 lbs.	43 lbs.	16.00	16.00
1 30	26 lbs.	26 lbs.	7.00	7.00
1 60	$1\frac{3}{4}$ lbs.	$1\frac{3}{4}$ lbs.	.50	.50
1 62	$3\frac{1}{4}$ lbs.	$3\frac{1}{4}$ lbs.	1.00	1.00
1 64	$7\frac{1}{2}$ lbs.	$7\frac{1}{2}$ lbs.	2.20	2.20
1 67	36 lbs.	36 lbs.	5.00	5.00
2 87	$5\frac{1}{2}$ lbs.	11 lbs.	4.75	9.50
1 88	9 lbs.	9 lbs.	5.25	5.25
1 89	16 lbs.	16 lbs.	6.00	6.00
1 90	$26\frac{1}{2}$ lbs.	$26\frac{1}{2}$ lbs.	7.00	7.00
1 628	35 lbs.	35 lbs.	8.50	8.50
2 677	$7\frac{1}{2}$ lbs.	15 lbs.	5.75	11.50
1 678	$11\frac{1}{2}$ lbs.	$11\frac{1}{2}$ lbs.	6.50	6.50
1 679	$18\frac{1}{2}$ lbs.	$18\frac{1}{2}$ lbs.	7.50	7.50
1 680	$30\frac{1}{2}$ lbs.	$30\frac{1}{2}$ lbs.	8.75	8.75
1 681	48 lbs.	48 lbs.	10.50	10.50
35		$416\frac{3}{4}$		$161.15

In the above assortment of Simpson Quick Acting, Standard and Six Hundred Line Vises, we have included the most salable sizes for the average dealer. The largest Vise in the list has 4" jaws.

ATHOL MACHINE COMPANY

D ## VISE DISPLAY STAND

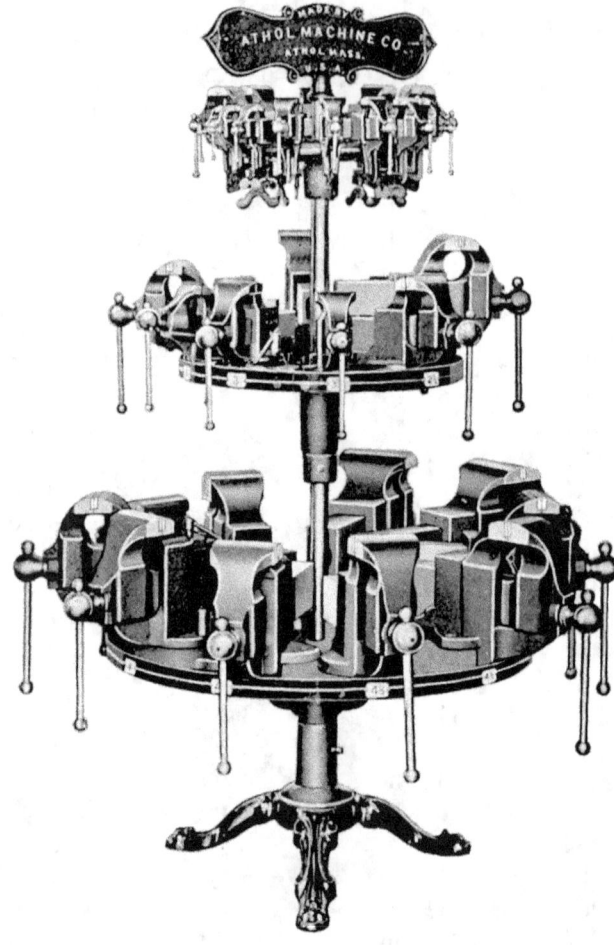

No. D
With Three Shelves for Floor Display of Standard, Six Hundred Line and Simpson Vises

Height, 57 in.; extreme dia. with Vises, 45 in.

For Domestic Shipment

Weight of Stand, crated, 143 lbs. Total weight of shipment, including Vises, 935 lbs.

For Ocean Shipment

Weight of Stand, boxed, net 125 lbs., gross 190 lbs.

Total weight of shipment, including Vises, net 890 lbs., gross 1050 lbs.

Total measurement of 5 cases, 23.39 cu. ft.

Every Vise fully warranted—See Page 2. Prices and full information given upon request.

ATHOL VISES AND TOOLS, ATHOL, MASS., U. S. A.

ATHOL MACHINE COMPANY

ATHOL VISES

LIST OF SIMPSON, STANDARD AND SIX HUNDRED LINE VISES SENT WITH VISE DISPLAY STAND No. D.

No. Vises	Weight Each	Total Weight	List Each	Total List
3 0	1½ lbs.	4½ lbs.	$1.25	$3.75
2 1	2¾ lbs.	5½ lbs.	1.75	3.50
3 2	5¾ lbs.	17¼ lbs.	2.75	8.25
2 3	1½ lbs.	3 lbs.	1.40	2.80
2 4	2¾ lbs.	5½ lbs.	2.00	4.00
1 5	5¾ lbs.	5¾ lbs.	3.15	3.15
1 11	9½ lbs.	9½ lbs.	6.50	6.50
1 14	44 lbs.	44 lbs.	10.50	10.50
1 29	15½ lbs.	15½ lbs.	6.00	6.00
1 42	48 lbs.	48 lbs.	11.00	11.00
1 60	1¾ lbs.	1¾ lbs.	.50	.50
1 62	3¼ lbs.	3¼ lbs.	1.00	1.00
1 64	7½ lbs.	7½ lbs.	2.20	2.20
1 72	34 lbs	34 lbs.	5.00	5.00
1 88	9 lbs.	9 lbs.	5.25	5.25
1 89	16 lbs.	16 lbs.	6.00	6.00
1 629	30 lbs.	30 lbs.	7.00	7.00
1 91	38 lbs.	38 lbs.	8.50	8.50
1 92	50 lbs.	50 lbs.	10.00	10.00
1 93	65 lbs.	65 lbs.	13.00	13.00
1 147	61 lbs.	61 lbs.	22.00	22.00
1 677	7½ lbs.	7½ lbs.	5.75	5.75
1 678	11½ lbs.	11½ lbs	6.50	6.50
1 679	18½ lbs.	18½ lbs.	7.50	7.50
1 628	35 lbs.	35 lbs.	8.50	8.50
1 680	30½ lbs.	30½ lbs.	8.75	8.75
1 681	48 lbs.	48 lbs.	10.50	10.50
1 683	83½ lbs.	83½ lbs.	16.00	16.00
35		708½		$203.40

This assortment of our Simpson Quick Acting, Six Hundred Line and Standard Vises includes the most salable sizes up to a 5" jaw vise.

ATHOL VISES AND TOOLS, ATHOL, MASS., U. S. A

ATHOL VISES
The Starrett Improved Vise

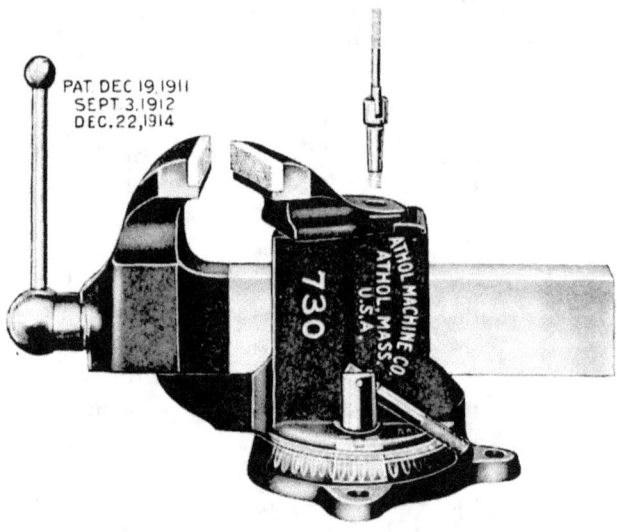

We present the Starrett Improved Patented Vise, not as an experiment, but as a fully worked out improvement in a tool that has never had the attention paid to it that it merits, considering the important place it occupies in every factory.

The Starrett Vise has a clutch in the handle which works like a ratchet, and the swivel base has the only positive lock made.

The handle does not slide through the screw head. It will stay in any position you place it. A spring fastener bearing against the under side of the head holds it there. You tighten the jaws on the work and then turn the handle, without turning the screw, to any position where it will be out of the way. You just pull out the screw head a little, with a perfectly natural movement of the hand, leaving the handle where you want it and the handle at once automatically engages with the screw. The man who works all day placing duplicate parts in his vise will readily appreciate the advantages of this improvement; moreover, you can tighten the jaws on the work more firmly than with any other device because you can select, at will, just the point where you can take advantage of the greatest leverage.

The shank of the swivel jaw is made very heavy and has a square keyway and a square key long enough to give a good bearing. The taper pin is made with a straight threaded end so that it can be drawn into place and, at the same time, be easily removed when desired.

This vise is in a class by itself, embodying more improvements than have been made in vises for many years.

ATHOL VISES

701
703

STARRETT'S IMPROVED VISE

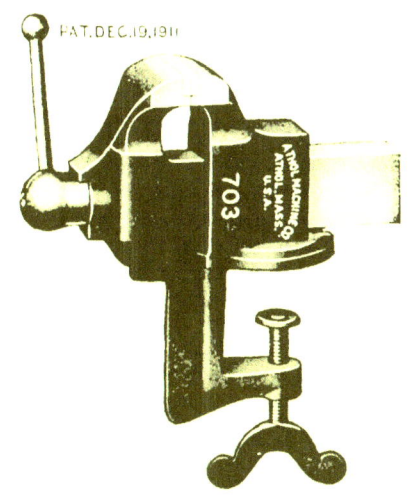

JEWELERS' AND ARTISANS' CLAMP VISE

With Patent Adjustable Handle

This vise is particularly adapted for the use of any factory where there is a good deal of small duplicate work, owing to the fact that the handle can be placed in the best position for opening or closing the vise, thus assuring quickness of action.

Can be carried in the tool box of an automobile and clamped to the running board for a quick repair. It will prove the most useful tool in the kit.

Fully warranted — See Page 2.

Number	Width Jaws	Jaws Open	Weight	Price
701	$1\frac{5}{8}$ in.	$1\frac{3}{4}$ in.	$2\frac{3}{4}$ lbs.	$2.50
703	$2\frac{1}{8}$ in.	2 in.	6 lbs.	3.50

Furnished with smooth faced, tempered steel jaws.

705
707
709
711
713
715
717
719
721

ATHOL VISES
STARRETT'S IMPROVED VISE

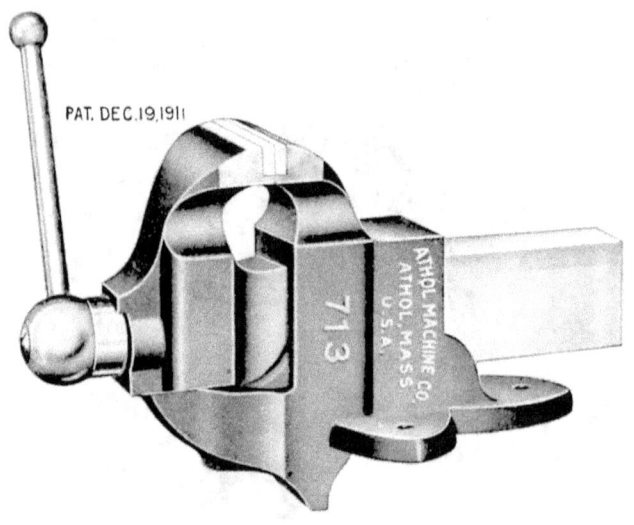

MACHINISTS' STATIONARY BASE VISE
With Patent Adjustable Handle

Fully warranted—See Page 2

Number	Width Jaws	Jaws Open	Weight	Price
705	2⅛ in.	2 in.	6 lbs.	$4.75
707	2½ in.	2¾ in.	10 lbs.	5.25
709	3 in.	3½ in.	16½ lbs.	6.00
711	3½ in.	4 in.	27 lbs.	7.00
713	4 in.	5 in.	40 lbs.	8.50
715	4½ in.	6 in.	54 lbs.	10.00
717	5 in.	7 in.	68 lbs.	13.00
719	5½ in.	9½ in.	97 lbs.	18.50
721	6 in.	10½ in.	135 lbs.	25.00

No. 705 has smooth-faced, tempered steel jaws. Other numbers will be furnished with check jaws unless smooth jaws are specified.

ATHOL VISES
STARRETT'S IMPROVED VISE

704
706
708
710
712
714
716
718
720

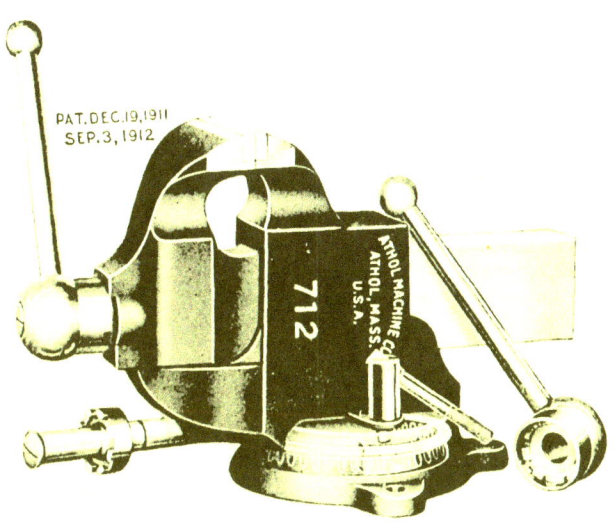

MACHINISTS' SWIVEL BASE VISE
With Patent Adjustable Handle
Fully warranted—See Page 2

Number	Width Jaws	Jaws Open	Weight	Price
704	$2\frac{1}{8}$ in.	2 in.	$7\frac{1}{2}$ lbs.	$5.75
706	$2\frac{1}{2}$ in.	$2\frac{3}{4}$ in.	$11\frac{1}{2}$ lbs.	6.50
708	3 in.	$3\frac{1}{2}$ in.	19 lbs.	7.50
710	$3\frac{1}{2}$ in.	4 in.	31 lbs.	8.75
712	4 in.	5 in.	49 lbs.	10.50
714	$4\frac{1}{2}$ in.	6 in.	66 lbs.	12.50
716	5 in.	7 in.	85 lbs.	16.00
718	$5\frac{1}{2}$ in.	$9\frac{1}{2}$ in.	112 lbs.	22.00
720	6 in.	$10\frac{1}{2}$ in.	155 lbs.	30.00

No. 704 has smooth-faced, tempered steel jaws. Other numbers will be furnished with check jaws unless smooth jaws are specified.

ATHOL VISES

STARRETT'S IMPROVED VISE

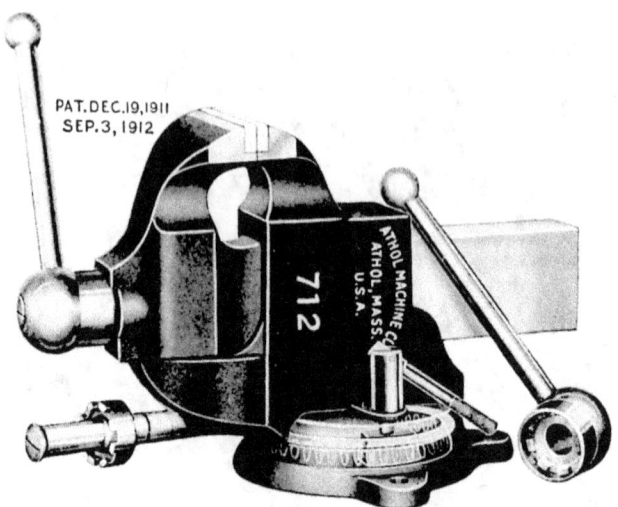

SWIVEL BASE VISE

This vise has all the improved features of the stationary base vise and has in addition the improved locking device which consists of a bolt, with a corrugated head, engaging a correspondingly corrugated base fastened to the bench. Loosening the nut on the bolt releases the corrugated connection, when the vise can be swiveled to any desired angle and quickly locked by turning the nut connected with the lever handle. Holding the lever upright the nut can be speedily rotated by thumb and finger, then dropped and used to give the locking grip which will hold firmly.

It is the only swivel base on the market which cannot be slipped after the clamp nut is tightened by the hand. You can pull the bolts out of the bench or break the ears off the side of the vise, and even then the swivel base will not slip. This swivel base vise is as solid as a stationary base vise.

Prices, etc., shown on Page 17.

ATHOL VISES

STARRETT'S IMPROVED VISE

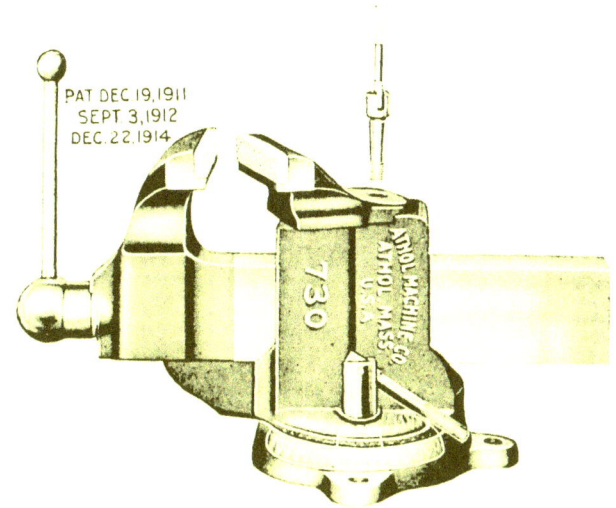

SWIVEL BASE AND SWIVEL JAW VISE

The swivel jaw on this vise contains some entirely new features. The heavy, carefully fitted shank is made with a square keyway and a key long enough to give a proper bearing, while the shape insures long wear and prevents jamming. It is a regular machine construction.

The taper locking pin, fully covered by patent, is made with a straight threaded end so that it can be drawn down to a proper bearing and can be easily removed when it is desired to make use of the swivel jaw.

Contrast this with the plain taper pin so long in use, which required a hammer or wrench to loosen, and could never be depended upon to hold the jaw tight.

This line of vises also has the patent adjustable handle as shown and described on Page 14, and the patent positive lock swivel base, fully described and illustrated on Page 18.

See next two pages for prices, etc.

725
727
729
731
733
735
737

ATHOL VISES
STARRETT'S IMPROVED VISE

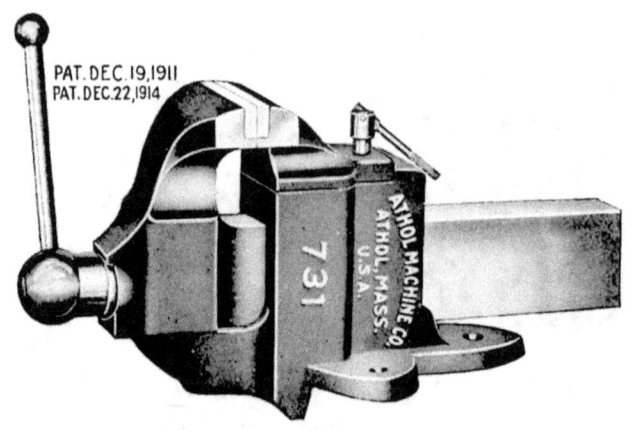

MACHINISTS' STATIONARY BASE AND SWIVEL JAW VISE
With Patent Adjustable Handle
Fully warranted—See Page 2

Number	Width Jaws	Jaws Open	Weight	Price
725	2½ in.	3½ in.	17 lbs.	$7.00
727	3 in.	4 in.	21 lbs.	8.00
729	3½ in.	5 in.	31 lbs.	9.00
731	4 in.	6 in.	42 lbs.	11.25
733	4½ in.	7 in.	57 lbs.	13.25
735	5 in.	8 in.	74 lbs.	17.50
737	5½ in.	9 in.	93 lbs.	21.25

Check-faced, tempered steel jaws will be furnished unless smooth-faced jaws are specified.

ATHOL VISES

STARRETT'S IMPROVED VISE

724
726
728
730
732
734
736

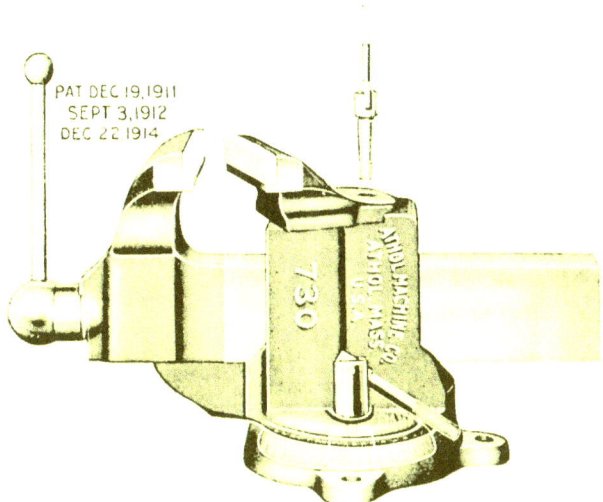

MACHINISTS' SWIVEL BASE AND SWIVEL JAW VISE

With Patent Adjustable Handle

Fully warranted — See Page 2

Number	Width Jaws	Jaws Open	Weight	Price
724	$2\frac{1}{2}$ in.	$3\frac{1}{2}$ in.	18 lbs.	$8.50
726	3 in.	4 in.	23 lbs.	9.50
728	$3\frac{1}{2}$ in.	5 in.	36 lbs.	10.75
730	4 in.	6 in.	49 lbs.	13.25
732	$4\frac{1}{2}$ in.	7 in.	68 lbs.	15.75
734	5 in.	8 in.	87 lbs.	20.00
736	$5\frac{1}{2}$ in.	9 in.	108 lbs.	23.75

Check-faced, tempered steel jaws will be furnished unless smooth faced jaws are specified.

ATHOL   MACHINE   COMPANY

ATHOL VISES

SIX HUNDRED LINE
Patented

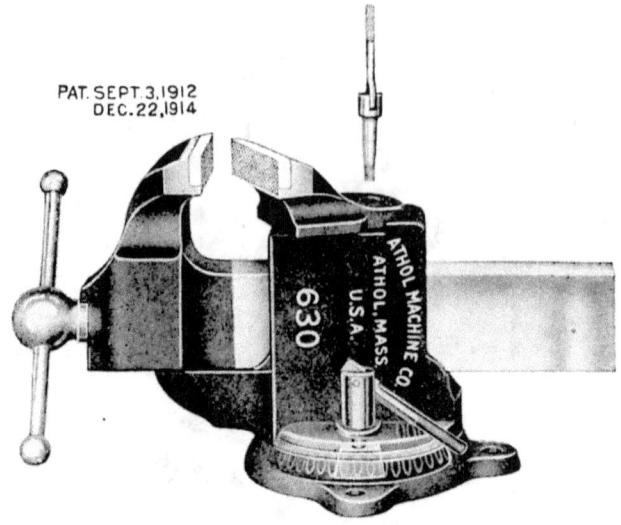

SWIVEL BASE AND SWIVEL JAW VISE

For many years vise manufacturers have endeavored to make a swivel base vise that would operate quickly and easily, and yet stay where it was clamped when subjected to unusual strain.

In our Six Hundred Line we are furnishing a positive lock, swivel base vise that can be depended upon to stay exactly where it is clamped until the bench gives way.

The locking device consists of a bolt with a corrugated head, engaging a correspondingly corrugated base that is fastened to the bench. Loosening the lever will allow the bolt head to drop down and release the connection, when the vise can be swivelled to any desired angle and quickly locked.

Simple, quick to operate, and most effective.

The same style of Swivel Jaw is used on the Six Hundred Line as on the Starrett Improved Patented Vises described on Page 19. The taper pin with a straight threaded end for quick removal. Also the square keyway with a long bearing.

ATHOL VISES AND TOOLS, ATHOL, MASS., U. S. A.

ATHOL VISES
SIX HUNDRED LINE

677
678
679
680
681
682
683
684
685
686
687

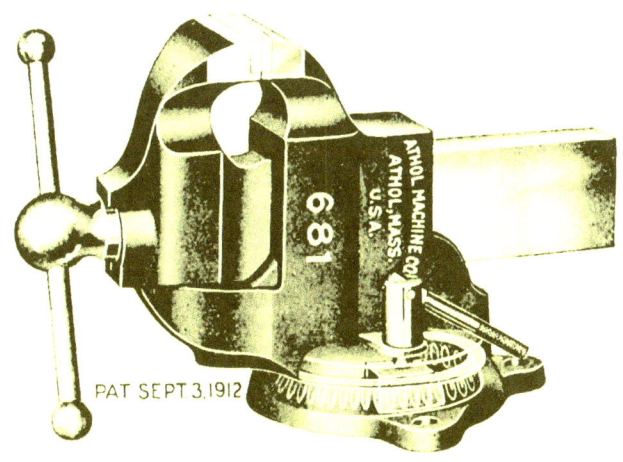

MACHINISTS' SWIVEL BASE VISE
Fully warranted — See Page 2

Vise No.	Width Jaw	Jaws Open	Weight	Price
677	2⅛ in.	2 in.	7½ lbs.	$5.75
678	2½ in.	2¾ in.	11½ lbs.	6.50
679	3 in.	3½ in.	18½ lbs.	7.50
680	3½ in.	4 in.	30½ lbs.	8.75
681	4 in.	5 in.	48 lbs.	10.50
682	4½ in.	6 in.	64½ lbs.	12.50
683	5 in.	7 in.	83½ lbs.	16.00
SWIVEL BASE EXTRA HEAVY CHIPPING VISE				
684	5½ in.	9½ in.	116 lbs.	$22.00
685	6 in.	10½ in.	155 lbs.	30.00
686	7 in.	12½ in.	200 lbs.	42.50
687	8 in.	12½ in.	275 lbs.	55.00

No. 677 has smooth-faced, tempered steel jaws.

Nos. 679, 680, 681 and 682 will be furnished with smooth jaws when so ordered, at no extra cost.

Nos. 678, 683, 684, 685, 686 and 687 have checked jaws.

625
627
629
631
633
635
637

ATHOL VISES

SIX HUNDRED LINE

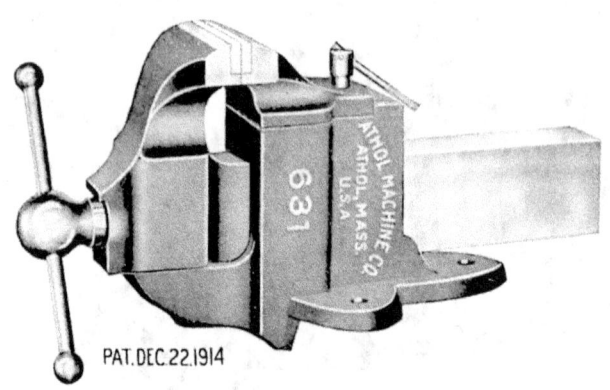

MACHINISTS' STATIONARY BASE AND SWIVEL JAW VISE

Fully Warranted—See Page 2

Number	Width Jaw	Jaws Open	Weight	Price
625	2½ in.	3½ in.	17 lbs.	$5.50
627	3 in.	4 in.	21 lbs.	6.25
629	3½ in.	5 in.	30 lbs.	7.00
631	4 in.	6 in.	41 lbs.	9.00
633	4½ in.	7 in.	57 lbs.	10.50
635	5 in.	8 in.	74 lbs.	14.00
637	5½ in.	9 in.	93 lbs.	17.00

Will be furnished with check-faced, tempered steel jaws unless smooth-faced jaws are specified.

Swivel Jaw construction same as that of the Starrett Vise fully described on Page 19.

The taper pin has a straight threaded end so that it may be drawn down to give a proper bearing and, at the same time, be readily removed.

ATHOL VISES
SIX HUNDRED LINE

624
626
628
630
632
634
636

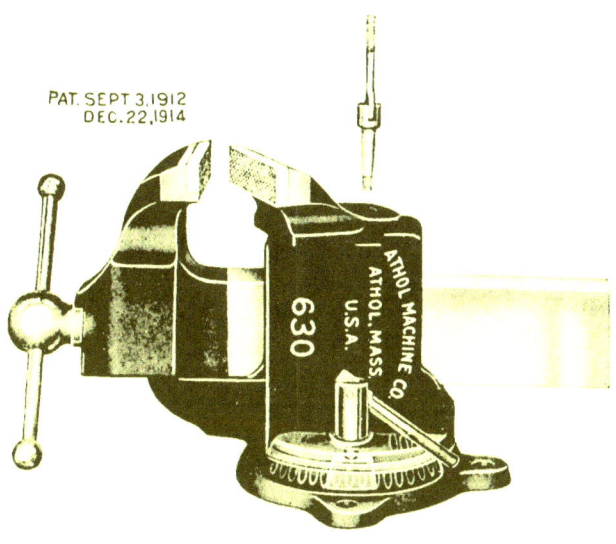

MACHINISTS' SWIVEL BASE AND SWIVEL JAW VISE
Fully warranted—See Page 2

Number	Width Jaw	Jaws Open	Weight	Price
624	2½ in.	3½ in.	18 lbs.	$6.75
626	3 in.	4 in.	23 lbs.	7.50
628	3½ in.	5 in.	35 lbs.	8.50
630	4 in.	6 in.	48 lbs.	10.50
632	4½ in.	7 in.	68 lbs.	12.50
634	5 in.	8 in.	87 lbs.	16.00
636	5½ in.	9 in.	108 lbs.	19.00

Will be furnished with check-faced, tempered steel jaws unless smooth-faced jaws are specified.

Swivel Jaw construction same as that of the Starrett Vise fully described on Page 19.

The Swivel Base that can be tightened by hand so that it is impossible for it to slip, and that can be as readily released when desired, is described in detail on pages 18 and 22.

87
88
89
90
91
92
93
94
95
96
97

ATHOL VISES
STANDARD LINE

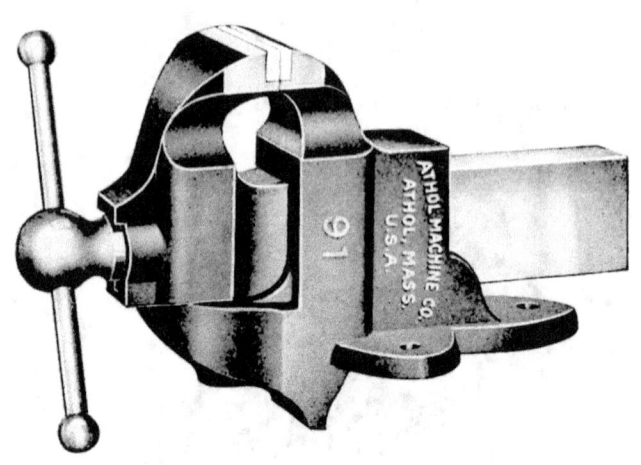

MACHINISTS' STATIONARY BASE VISE
Fully warranted—See Page 2

Number	Width Jaw	Jaws Open	Weight	Price
87	2 1/8 in.	2 in.	5 1/2 lbs.	$4.75
88	2 1/2 in.	2 3/4 in.	9 lbs.	5.25
89	3 in.	3 1/2 in.	16 lbs.	6.00
90	3 1/2 in.	4 in.	26 1/2 lbs.	7.00
91	4 in.	5 in.	38 lbs.	8.50
92	4 1/2 in.	6 in.	50 lbs.	10.00
93	5 in.	7 in.	65 lbs.	13.00

STATIONARY BASE EXTRA HEAVY CHIPPING VISE

94	5 1/2 in.	8 in.	100 lbs.	$18.50
95	6 in.	9 in.	135 lbs.	25.00
96	7 in.	10 1/2 in.	190 lbs.	37.50
97	8 in.	12 1/2 in.	260 lbs.	50.00

No. 87 has smooth-faced, tempered steel jaws.

Nos. 89, 90, 91 and 92 will be furnished with smooth jaws when so ordered, at no extra cost.

Nos. 88, 93, 94, 95, 96 and 97 have checked jaws.

ATHOL VISES

STANDARD LINE

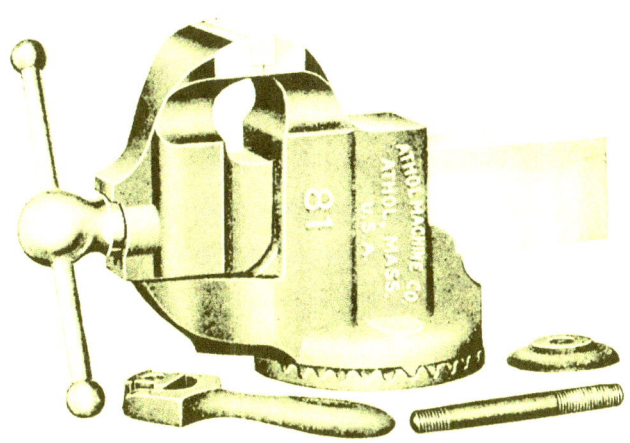

MACHINISTS' SWIVEL BASE BENCH VISE

Fully warranted — See Page 2

Number	Width Jaws	Jaws Open	Weight	Price
77	$2^{1}/_{8}$ in.	2 in.	$6^{1}/_{4}$ lbs.	$5.75
78	$2^{1}/_{2}$ in.	$2^{3}/_{4}$ in.	$9^{1}/_{2}$ lbs.	6.50
79	3 in.	$3^{1}/_{2}$ in.	18 lbs.	7.50
80	$3^{1}/_{2}$ in.	4 in.	$28^{1}/_{2}$ lbs.	8.75
81	4 in.	5 in.	45 lbs.	10.50
82	$4^{1}/_{2}$ in.	6 in.	60 lbs.	12.50
83	5 in.	7 in.	80 lbs.	16.00

No. 77 has smooth-faced, tempered steel jaws.

Nos. 79, 80, 81 and 82 will be furnished with smooth jaws when so ordered, at no extra cost.

Nos. 78 and 83 have checked jaws.

ATHOL VISES
STANDARD LINE

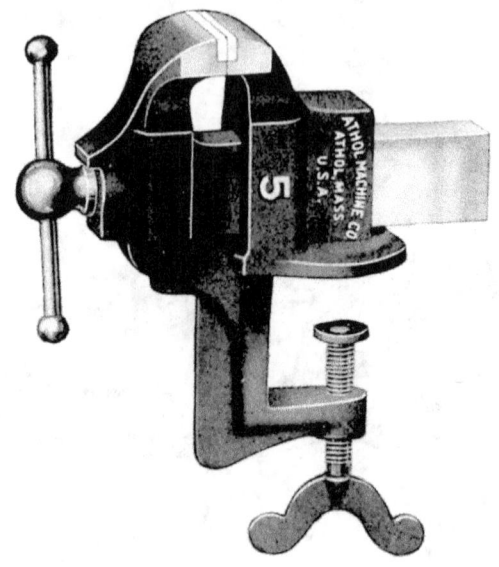

JEWELERS' AND ARTISANS' CLAMP VISE

Vise No. 5 is admirably adapted to attach to the running board of an automobile or seat of a motor boat for a quick repair. This also applies to No. 2, Page 35, and No. 703, Page 15.

Fully warranted—See Page 2

Number	Width Jaws	Jaws Open	Weight	Price
3	$1\frac{1}{8}$ in.	$1\frac{1}{4}$ in.	$1\frac{1}{2}$ lbs.	$1.40
4	$1\frac{5}{8}$ in.	$1\frac{3}{4}$ in.	$2\frac{3}{4}$ lbs.	2.00
5	$2\frac{1}{8}$ in.	2 in.	$5\frac{3}{4}$ lbs.	3.15
6	$1\frac{5}{8}$ in.	$1\frac{3}{4}$ in.	$2\frac{3}{4}$ lbs.	2.00

Furnished with smooth-faced, tempered steel jaws. No. 6 is the same as No. 4, except the clamp, which is extra long so it may be attached to a $2\frac{1}{4}$" bench.

ATHOL TAPER ATTACHMENTS

192
193

Single and Double Adjustable Taper
Attachments for Vises

No. 192

No. 193

These **attachments** allow the Mechanic to hold, in an ordinary vise, any style of taper work. **Short tapers** that it has been impossible to hold by means of a swivel jaw can be drilled or filed while held in a horizontal position. It is the only method of holding any taper piece in a **vertical** position. A pair of the **No. 192's** can be fitted to a drill vise and used to hold taper pieces for drilling in the end.

No. 192

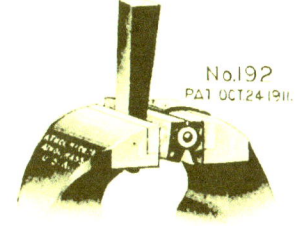

No. 193

We feel that every Toolmaker and Machinist will perceive the utility of these **attachments**. Write for discounts.

In ordering specify width of vise jaws and whether No. 192 or No. 193 is wanted.

Width Jaw	Price	Width Jaw	Price
1⅝ in.	$1.00	3 in.	$1.80
2⅛ in.	1.20	3½ in.	2.10
2½ in.	1.50	4 in.	2.40

ATHOL VISES AND TOOLS, ATHOL, MASS., U. S. A.

ATHOL VISES

THE SIMPSON PATENT QUICK-ADJUSTING PARALLEL VISE

THE SIMPLEST AND THE BEST QUICK-ADJUSTING VISE IN THE WORLD

This Vise is operated in the same manner as an ordinary screw vise, or it can be instantly opened or closed the full length, by a single movement of the hand, without the use of the screw, the screw being used merely to give the grip after adjusting the jaws to the work; thus combining a quick adjustment with all the advantages of the best screw vise—points not found combined in any other vise made.

By slightly raising the front jaw the screw and nut are disengaged; the jaw can then be moved in or out as may be required to adjust it to its work, and on removing the hand it instantly drops into place, the screw and nut again become engaged, and a single turn of the screw gives the required grip.

These vises are scientifically proportioned for the greatest strength and durability, as well as convenience in use, and there is no complicated mechanism, as in other quick-adjusting vises, to be constantly getting out of repair. Their extreme simplicity is one of their strongest features.

Note the completeness of this line, the sizes running from $1\frac{1}{8}$ in. to 5 in.

The constant and rapidly increasing demand for these vises is the best evidence of their superiority.

Every vise is fully warranted, and if one fails in any particular, by any reasonable usage, it will be replaced free of charge.

See Page 2.

ATHOL VISES
THE SIMPSON VISE
Quick Acting
JEWELERS' AND ARTISANS' CLAMP BASE VISE

0
1
2
10

These Vises have the quick acting feature as described on page 34.

Price list of clamp base vises.

Fully warranted — See Page 2

No.	Width Jaws	Jaws Open	Weight	Price
0	$1\frac{1}{8}$ in.	$1\frac{1}{4}$ in.	$1\frac{1}{2}$ lbs.	$1.25
1	$1\frac{5}{8}$ in.	$1\frac{3}{4}$ in.	$2\frac{3}{4}$ lbs.	1.75
2	$2\frac{1}{8}$ in.	2 in.	$5\frac{3}{4}$ lbs.	2.75

Furnished with smooth-faced, tempered steel jaws.

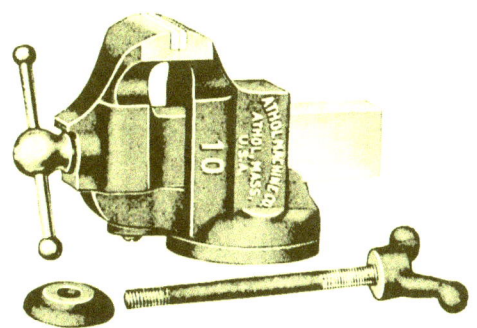

JEWELERS' AND ARTISANS' SWIVEL BASE VISE

Fully warranted — See Page 2

Number	Width Jaws	Jaws Open	Weight	Price
10	$2\frac{1}{8}$ in.	2 in.	$6\frac{1}{4}$ lbs.	$5.75

Furnished with smooth-faced, tempered steel jaws.

ATHOL VISES

THE SIMPSON VISE
Quick Acting

27
28
29
30
31
32
33

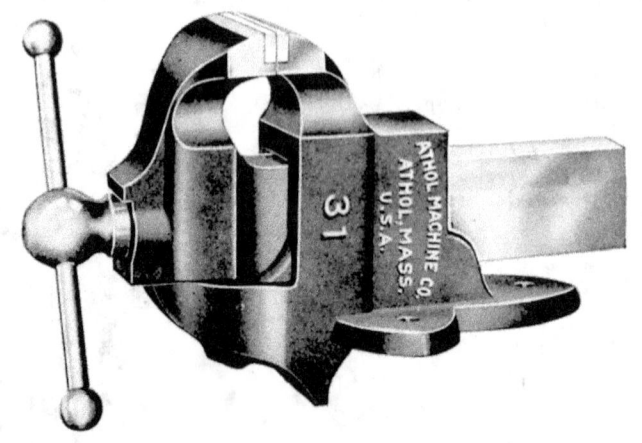

MACHINISTS' STATIONARY BASE BENCH VISE

Fully warranted—See Page 2

Number	Width Jaws	Jaws Open	Weight	Price
27	2 1/8 in.	2 in.	5 1/2 lbs.	$4.75
28	2 1/2 in.	2 3/4 in.	9 lbs.	5.25
29	3 in.	3 1/2 in.	15 1/2 lbs.	6.00
30	3 1/2 in.	4 in.	26 lbs.	7.00
31	4 in.	5 in.	37 lbs.	8.50
32	4 1/2 in.	5 3/4 in.	49 lbs.	10.00
33	5 in.	6 1/2 in.	64 lbs.	13.00

No. 27 has smooth-faced, tempered steel jaws.

Nos. 29, 30, 31 and 32 will be furnished with smooth jaws when so ordered, at no extra cost.

Nos. 28 and 33 have checked jaws.

ATHOL VISES

THE SIMPSON VISE

Quick Acting

11
12
13
14
15
16

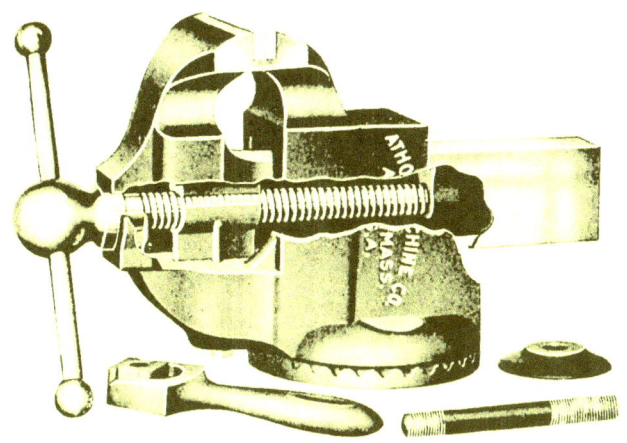

MACHINISTS' SWIVEL BASE BENCH VISE

Fully warranted — See Page 2

Number	Width Jaws	Jaws Open	Weight	Price
11	$2\frac{1}{2}$ in.	$2\frac{3}{4}$ in.	$9\frac{1}{2}$ lbs.	$6.50
12	3 in.	$3\frac{1}{2}$ in.	$17\frac{1}{2}$ lbs.	7.50
13	$3\frac{1}{2}$ in.	4 in.	28 lbs.	8.75
14	4 in.	5 in.	44 lbs.	10.50
15	$4\frac{1}{2}$ in.	$5\frac{3}{4}$ in.	59 lbs.	12.50
16	5 in.	$6\frac{1}{4}$ in.	78 lbs.	16.00

Nos. 12, 13, 14 and 15 will be furnished with smooth jaws when so ordered, at no extra cost.

Nos. 11 and 16 have checked jaws.

40
41

ATHOL VISES

THE SIMPSON VISE

Quick Acting

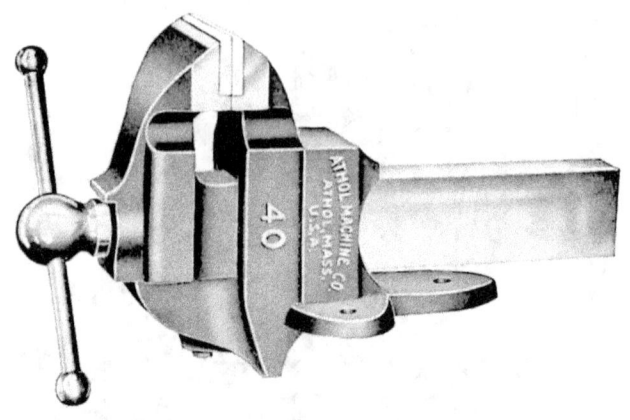

STATIONARY BASE, COACHMAKERS', CARPENTERS', AND PATTERN WORKERS' VISE

Fully warranted—See Page 2

Number	Width Jaws	Jaws Open	Weight	Price
40	4 in.	8½ in.	41 lbs.	$9.00
41	4½ in.	10½ in.	49 lbs.	10.00

Furnished with smooth-faced, tempered steel jaws.

The **Quick Acting** feature of these vises allows the front jaw to be drawn out to the full capacity instantly, and a single turn of the handle clamps the work firmly.

ATHOL VISES

THE SIMPSON VISE

Quick Acting

SWIVEL BASE, COACHMAKERS', CARPENTERS', AND PATTERN WORKERS' VISE.

Fully warranted—See Page 2

Number	Width Jaws	Jaws Open	Weight	Price
42	4 in.	$8\frac{1}{2}$ in.	48 lbs.	$11.00
43	$4\frac{1}{2}$ in.	$10\frac{1}{2}$ in.	58 lbs.	12.00

Furnished with smooth-faced, tempered steel jaws.

The simplicity of construction, in connection with the Quick Acting feature, commends these vises to all woodworkers.

145
147
149

ATHOL VISES

COMBINATION PIPE VISE

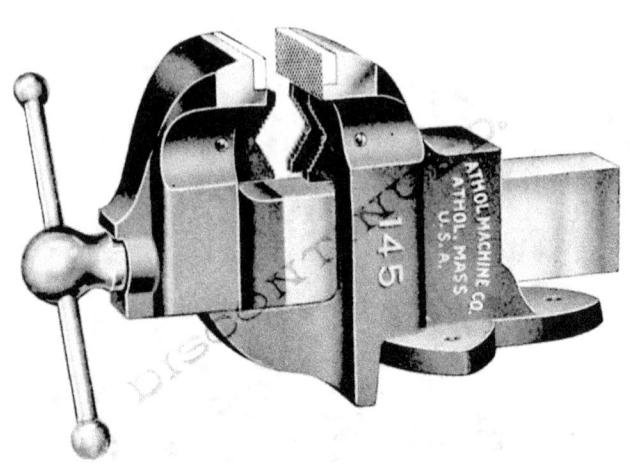

STATIONARY BASE

The front pipe jaw can be reversed when it becomes worn, giving double wear. A heavy duty vise.

Fully warranted—See Page 2

Number	Width Jaws	Jaws Open	Weight lbs.	Capacity Pipe, in.	Vises Each	Jaws, Set (3)
145	3¾ in.	5 in.	43	⅛ in. to 2½ in.	$16.00	$1.25
147	4½ in.	6 in.	61	⅛ in. to 3½ in.	22.00	1.50
149	5½ in.	7 in.	93	¼ in. to 4 in.	32.00	1.75

Furnished with check-faced, tempered steel jaws—renewable if specified.

ATHOL VISES

**144
146
148**

COMBINATION PIPE VISE

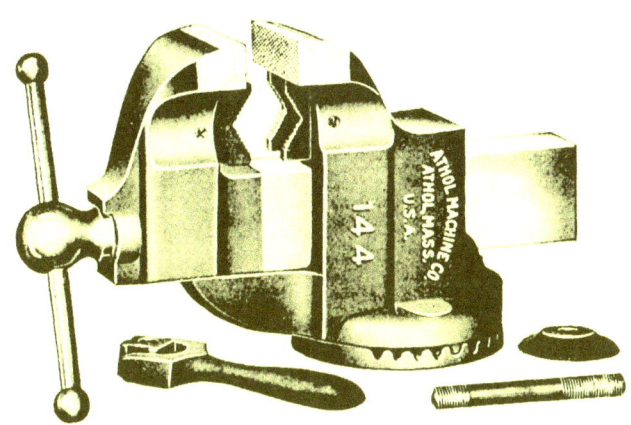

SWIVEL BASE

The front pipe jaw can be reversed when it becomes worn, giving double wear.

Fully warranted—See Page 2

Number	Width Jaws	Jaws Open	Weight lbs.	Capacity Pipe, in.	Vises Each	Jaws, Set (3)
144	$3\frac{3}{4}$ in.	5 in.	$48\frac{1}{2}$	$\frac{1}{8}$ in. to $2\frac{1}{2}$ in.	$16.00	$1.25
146	$4\frac{1}{2}$ in.	6 in.	70	$\frac{1}{8}$ in. to $3\frac{1}{2}$ in.	22.00	1.50
148	$5\frac{1}{2}$ in.	7 in.	100	$\frac{1}{4}$ in. to 4 in.	32.00	1.75

Furnished with check-faced, tempered steel jaws—renewable if specified.

150

ATHOL PIPE GRIPS

STANDARD PIPE GRIP

SWIVEL JAWS

		Price
No. 150 A.	Fits any 3 to 4½ in. Machinist's Vise, Will hold ¼ to 2½ in. pipe.	$2.50
No. 150 B.	Fits any 4¾ to 5½ in. Machinist's Vise, Will hold ¼ to 5 in. pipe.	2.75
No. 150 C.	Fits any 6 to 8½ in. Machinist's Vise, Will hold ¼ to 6 in. pipe.	3.00

There are probably but few tools that have to stand the hard usage of pipe vises and grips.

That we recognize this fact and still include them in our broad guarantee on Page 2 shows the care we have taken and the confidence we have in this line.

ATHOL VISES

AMATEUR VISE

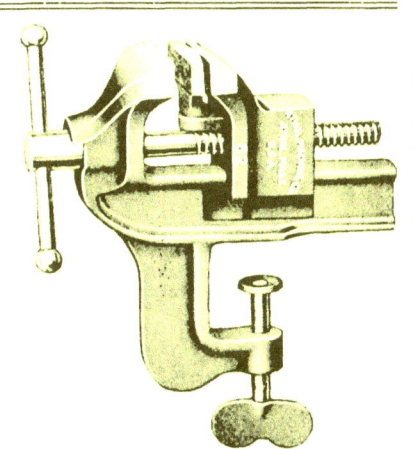

60
62
69
70
71
72

Fully warranted—See Page 2

Number	Width Jaws	Jaws Open	Weight	Price
60	1½ in.	1¾ in.	1¾ lbs.	$0.50
62	2 in.	2¼ in.	3¼ lbs.	1.00

Nos. 60 and 62 have steel jaws and wrought iron screws, and No. 62 has a steel swivel jaw attachment as shown in cut.

FARMERS' VISE

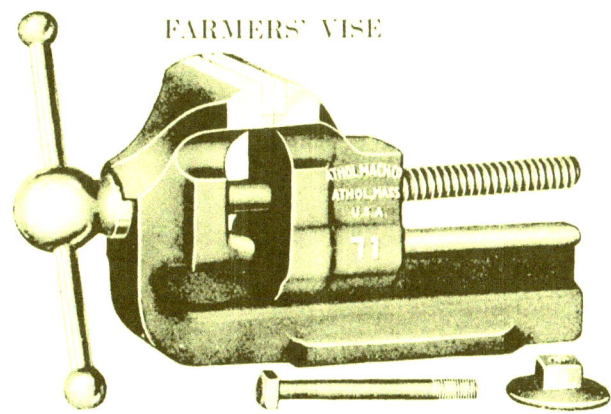

Number	Width Jaws	Jaws Open	Weight	Price
69	3 in.	3 in.	8 lbs.	$1.75
70	3½ in.	4 in.	12 lbs.	2.25
71	4 in.	5 in.	22 lbs.	3.50
72	4½ in.	6 in.	34 lbs.	5.00

Furnished with check-faced, tempered steel jaws.

These Vises are designed to meet the large and growing demand among farmers and others for a cheap, strong vise.

63
64
65
66
67

ATHOL VISES

OVAL SLIDE VISE

Made of best quality of stock and proportioned for strength and durability.

Fully warranted—See Page 2

Number	Width Jaws	Jaws Open	Weight	Price
63	2 in.	3 in.	7 lbs.	$1.70
64	2½ in.	3¼ in.	7½ lbs.	2.20
65	3 in.	4½ in.	16½ lbs.	3.00
66	3½ in.	5¾ in.	27 lbs.	3.80
67	4 in.	6¼ in.	36 lbs.	5.00

Furnished with check-faced, tempered steel jaws.

INSTRUCTIONS FOR ORDERING VISE PARTS

In ordering Extra Parts for vises be sure and give number cast in large figures on the side of back jaw and the width of the vise jaw. Also state whether the front, movable jaw or the back jaw which is fastened to the bench, is desired.

It is absolutely necessary that we have these particulars in order to send jaws that will fit.

Do not send us part of a broken vise jaw, and request us to send another like it. We make several vises of the same size, the jaws of which will not interchange, and we cannot always tell from broken parts what to send.

If the unbroken jaw is sent us, and the number of the vise given, we will fit a new jaw, and no charge will be made for fitting.

HOUSEHOLD GRINDSTONE
No. 154

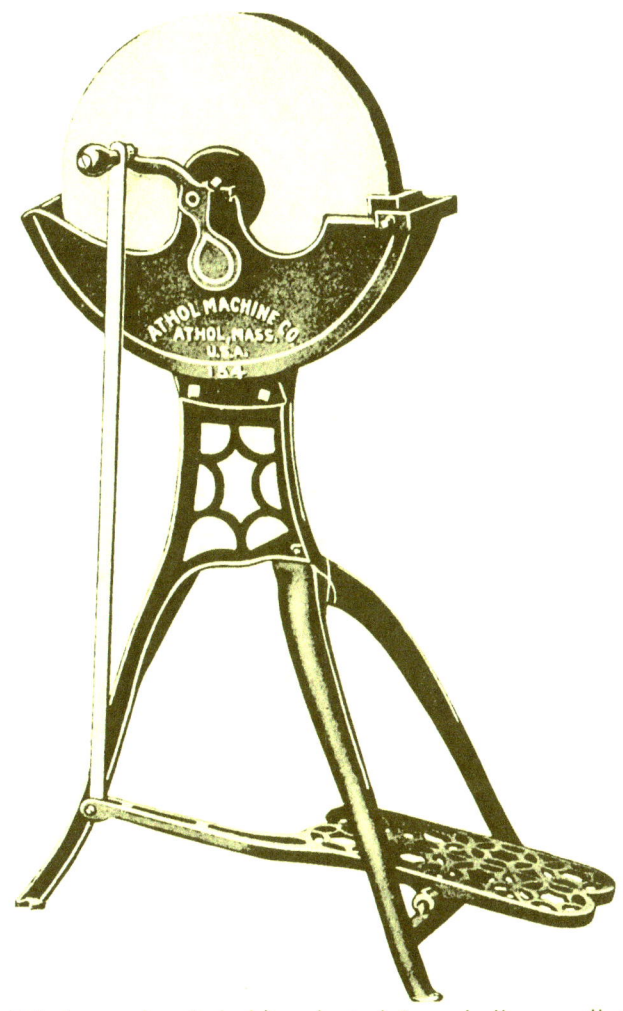

This Grindstone is admirably adapted for grinding small tools used by jewelers, amateur mechanics, etc., as well as for hotel or household purposes. The frame is strong and well made. The stone, 14 in. x $1\frac{3}{4}$ in., is carefully selected of the proper grit to do the work intended. Weight, 60 pounds.

Price each, $4.50.

ATHOL MACHINE COMPANY

155

IRON GRINDSTONE FRAME
No. 155

With adjustable tool rest, and truing attachment. Water guard will be furnished in place of truing attachment if specified.

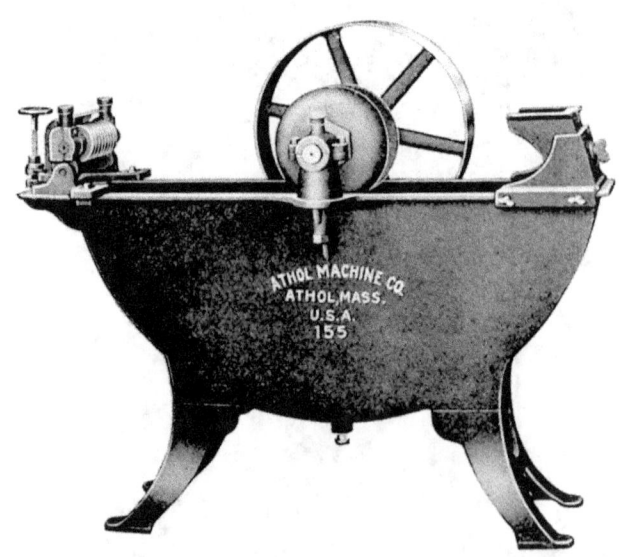

Weight, ready for shipment, 500 pounds
Pulley, 20 in. diameter, 5 in. face
Boxes Babbitt lined
Takes stone 42 in. diameter, 6 in. face
Price complete, without stone...................................$50.00
Price with stone quoted on request

ATHOL VISES AND TOOLS, ATHOL, MASS., U. S. A.

IRON GRINDSTONE FRAME
No. 156

With water guard and adjustable tool rest

Takes stone 30 in. diameter and 4 in. face

Boxes Babbitt lined

Weight ready for shipment, 170 pounds

PRICES

Frame as illustrated	$15.00
Plain frame, without pulley or treadle attachment	12.00
Pulley, 15 in. diameter, 3 in. face	1.50
Treadle	1.50

Pulley has removable handle attached, as shown in cut

Price with stone quoted on request

IRON GRINDSTONE FRAME
No. 157

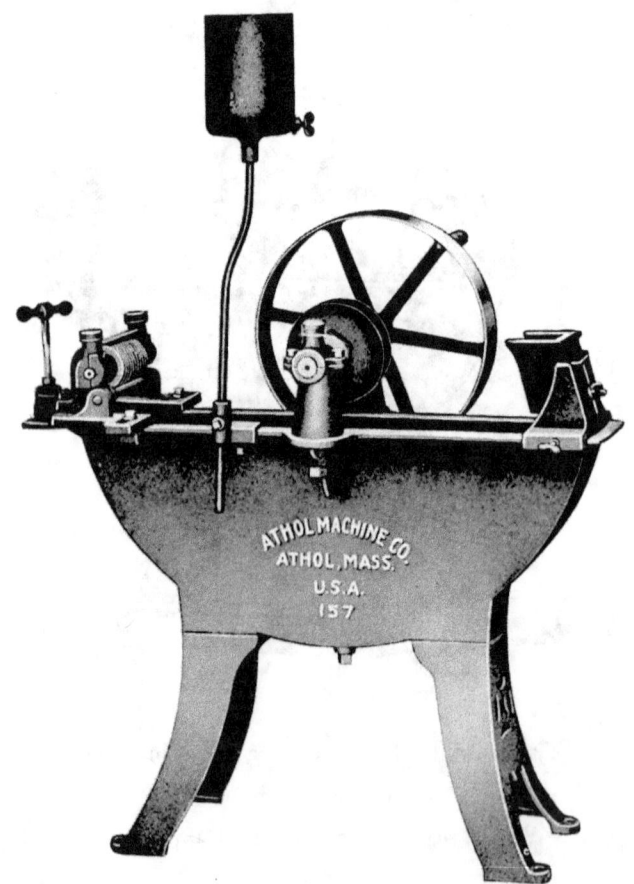

With adjustable tool rest, truing attachment, and waterpot
Takes stone 30 in. diameter and 4 in. face
Boxes Babbitt lined
Weight ready for shipment, 175 pounds

Price complete, as illustrated.................................$18.00
Without waterpot.. 17.00
Price with stone quoted on request

ADJUSTABLE GRINDSTONE TRUER
No. 161

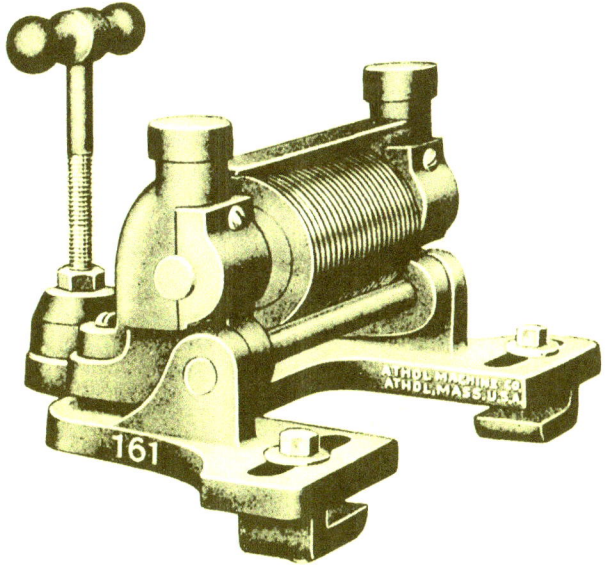

Can be used on any iron frame with flange and not over 14½ in. wide. The efficiency and durability of a grindstone depend upon the face being kept true. You cannot afford to pay a mechanic to stand and true up a stone when you can buy this device for so little money. With this the constant attention of a man is not required. Turn down the adjusting screw, turn on the water, and the Truer does the rest. No dust flying all over the room. A perfect face on the stone all the time. No gouging the stone by a tool slipping from the workman's hand.

The steel cutters are set on the arbor at a sharp angle. The Truer leaves the stone with a straight, even face and the gritty surface necessary for good grinding.

PRICES

No. 161 A—Adjustable to fit frames from 6½ in. to 10 in. wide, for stones of 2 in. to 4 in. face, length of cutting roll, 5 in. $7.50

Extra cutting roll.. 4.00

No. 161 B—Adjustable to fit frames from 9½ in. to 14½ in. wide, for stones of 4 in. to 6 in. face, length of cutting roll, 8 in. $15.00

Extra cutting roll.. 7.50

BENCH GRINDER
No. 158

158

This is a neat, rigid and practical grinder for bench use. As it occupies only a very small space, 9⅝ in. x 5 in. over all, height 7 in., a number of them may be located in different situations in a factory, thus effecting a considerable saving in workmen's time, which is a great advantage, especially when the slight cost of the grinders is considered.

The Drive Pulley is grooved for a round belt so it can be driven by motor if desired.

This tool is indispensable for grinding drills, reamers, counterbores, and a hundred and one small tools as well as for rough grinding of small machine parts, castings and forgings. All parts are painted or polished.

Size of base, 6 in. x 5 in. Length of spindle, 9⅝ in.

Height to center of spindle, 5⅝ in. Total height, 7 in.

Length of each bearing, 2¼ in. Diameter of spindle in bearing, ¾ in. Diameter of spindle for wheel, ½ in.

Distance between wheels, 6⅝ in. Diameter of flanges, 2¾ in. Width of pulley, 1⅝ in. Diameter of pulley, 2 in.

Size of emery wheels, 8 in. Nuts on spindle, case hardened, hexagon, 1 in.

Equipped with patent oil cups for bearings. Weight, 10 lbs.

For countershaft, see Page 53. Each grinder neatly and securely packed for shipment.

Price, each, without emery wheels, $7.00.

BENCH GRINDER
No. 159

This grinder is identical with No. 158 on the preceding page, with the addition of adjustable rests, which can be used advantageously in grinding pieces alike, and may be quickly detached when not needed. Drive Pulley grooved for round belt so it can be driven by motor. Weight, 13 pounds. Each grinder neatly and securely packed for shipment.

For countershaft, see page 53.

Price, each, without emery wheels, $8.50.

160   BENCH GRINDER COUNTERSHAFT
No. 160

The illustration obviates the need of verbal description. The belt is shipped by a simple turn of the lever. Fitted with drip cups to collect surplus oil.

Distance of drop to lower edge of drive pulley, $13\frac{1}{2}$ in.

Drive pulley, 12 in. x 2 in. Tight and loose pulley, $3\frac{1}{2}$ in. x $1\frac{5}{8}$ in. Diameter of shaft, $\frac{7}{8}$ in. Length of shaft, 14 in. Weight, 26 lbs. Speed of counter, 530 revolutions.

Each countershaft neatly and securely packed for shipment.

Price, each, $8.00

ATHOL SAFETY FIRST!

The question of safety for our workmen has seemed to us to be of paramount importance, and some of the devices we have adopted may be of interest. These are not expensive to install, but have required some thought.

PAGE 50

VIEW 1. The dead end shafting guard, *painted red*, will prevent clothing from being caught while working near it.

VIEW 2. A press is a dangerous machine, even at its best, but the guards, *painted red*, shown in the illustration, help to make it safe.

VIEW 4. A cast iron gear case for an old fashioned lathe prevents the workman from seeing what gears are on the lathe, while the heavy wire with sheet iron edges can be hooked in place, and the gears are shown through them at all times. They are *painted red*.

VIEW 5. Over every place where there is danger, we post one of the Red Spot Safety First Signs (as shown in the center of the page) with its appeal to the men to "Help us make this shop safe for you," as our hardest task is to make the men themselves see that they must follow instructions and use the devices provided for their own safety.

ATHOL MACHINE CO.'S CLUB ROOM AND PLAYGROUNDS

PAGE 51

VIEWS 1 & 2. These show two views of the club room maintained for our men. This is not only a reading and card room for our people, but it is also at the disposal of the boys in the vicinity at any time from 4 to 9.30 p. m. Cards, dominoes and checkers are furnished by the company, as well as daily papers and magazines, a phonograph, and a constant supply of records.

VIEW 4. A playground for the neighborhood children, with a ball ground, swings, teeters, and a sand pile. Hundreds of children gather here during the summer, and many a hard fought ball game is pulled off by the older ones. Maybe some Big League star is being developed right here. Who knows?

VIEW 5. The flooded playground in winter showing part of it cleared off for skating. Even in cold weather it takes but little extra effort to make the playground a gathering place for all the youngsters where they can be out of danger, and still find plenty of enjoyment.

ATHOL MACHINE COMPANY

1. Club Room.   2. Club Room at Noon Hour
3. Stephen L. French, Gen'l Mgr.
4. Playgrounds in Summer   5. Playgrounds in Winter

ATHOL VISES AND TOOLS, ATHOL, MASS., U. S. A.

ATHOL MACHINE COMPANY

1. Section of Stock Room.   2. Guards and Bell for Elevator
3. Stock Rack
4. Guards for Crane Gear.   5. Guards to Save Fingers

ATHOL VISES AND TOOLS, ATHOL, MASS., U. S. A.

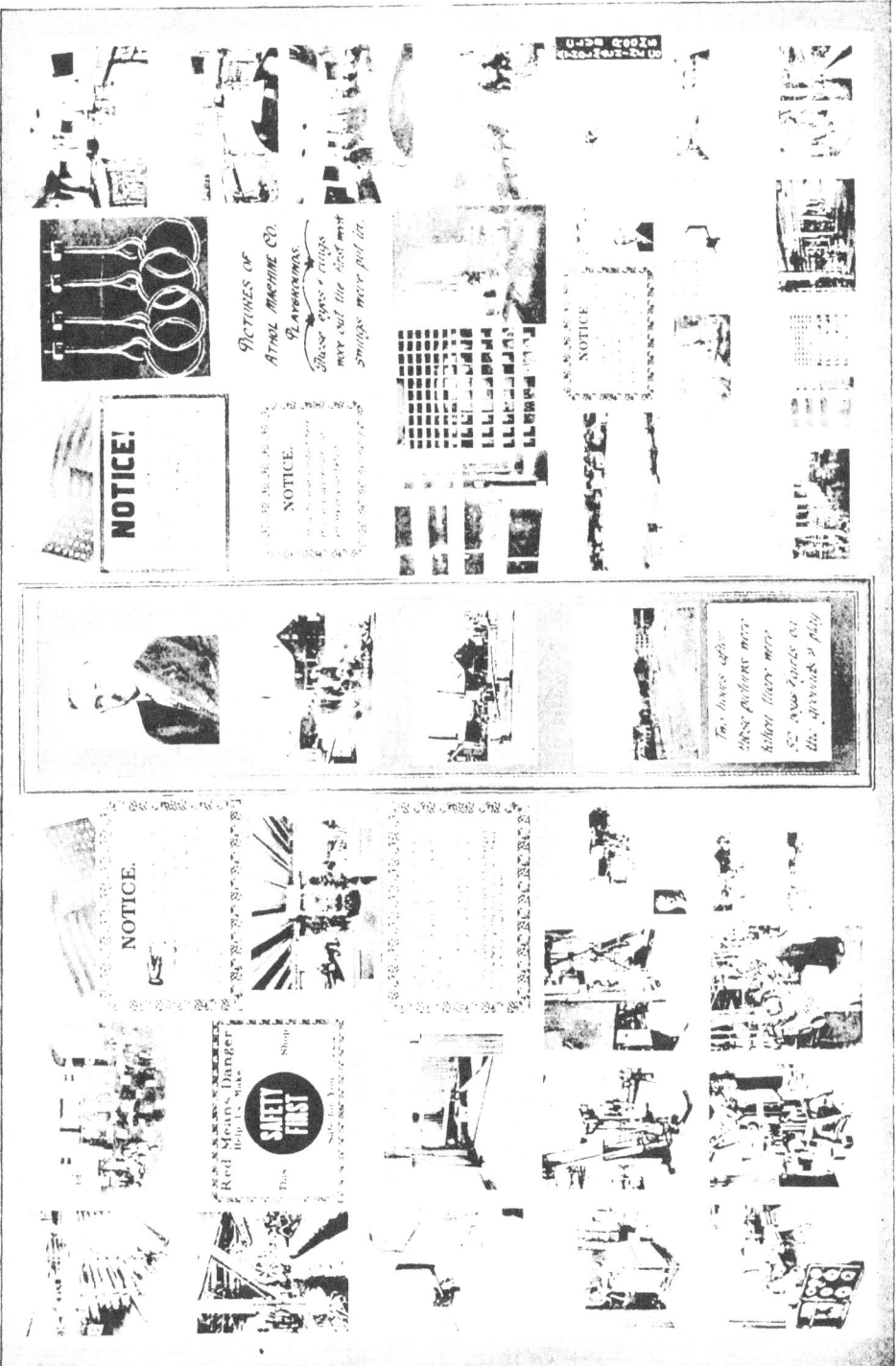

Display Board of Safety First, Playground, Club, Room and Shop Notices

ATHOL SAFETY FIRST!
PAGE 52

VIEW 1. This shows a corner of the stock room with some of the stock racks at the left, and some trucks loaded with finished Vises at the right.

VIEW 2. The top of the elevator is just coming flush with the floor. Note the two-leaved hinged top to prevent any object accidently dropped from a floor above, doing damage. This heavy wire mesh cover, being hinged, long plank or bar steel can be loaded when necessary.

VIEW 3. A section of a stock rack for finished parts. These are made double, to save space, with heavy wire screen between so the light will shine through from both sides.

VIEW 4. Part of the foundry showing guard over the crane gears. This guard is *painted red*, and in big white letters appears the warning "NEVER LEAVE CRANK ON CRANE OR PULL CRANE BY GEARS."

VIEW 5. Guard for a band saw. This is held in place by the tension of two spiral springs under the heads of the screws that pass through the vertical slot so it can be moved to the position desired. It is *painted red*.

DISPLAY BOARD
PAGE 53

This page shows a six by eight foot frame with photographs of the factory, playground, and club room, together with shop notices. It was made to fill a space on the wall of our offices, but caused so much favorable comment, indicating that welfare work need not be confined wholly to factories employing thousands of men, that we have been induced to include it as a part of some of our exhibits at various Trade and Welfare Exhibitions.

ATHOL TOOLS

PREMIER AND A. M. C.
SPRING CALIPERS AND DIVIDERS

These two styles of Calipers and Dividers, light and heavy, are made of the best material and by skilled workmen.

Our reputation as makers of the highest grade tools and machines for nearly fifty years is behind every tool.

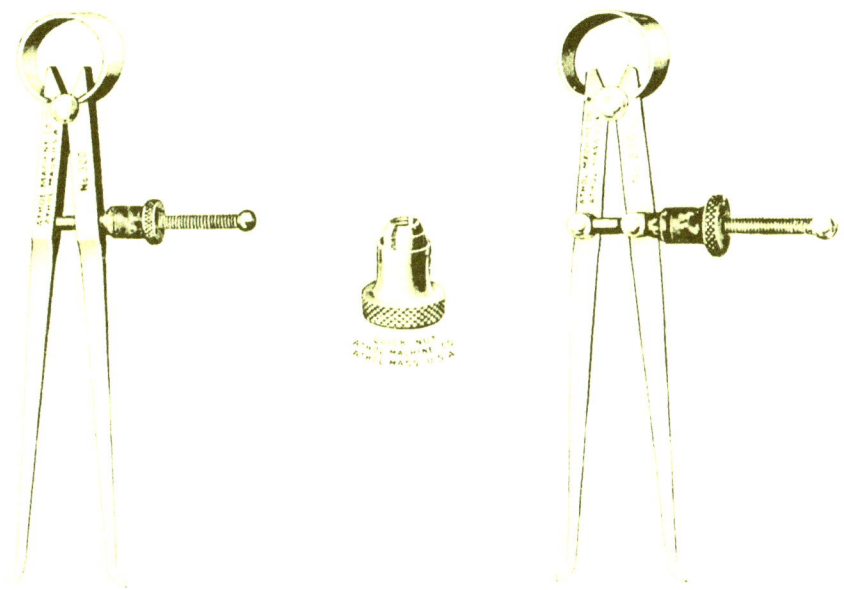

Athol Quick Nut Calipers and Dividers are made with a Quick Nut (as illustrated) which is positive in action, closing firmly on the screw at the slightest pressure. When the pressure is removed the Nut slides freely on the screw.

It is dust proof. It saves time. It is not expensive.

The Quick Acting feature does not detract from the appearance of the nut, it being as neat and attractive as the Solid Nut and the difference cannot be discerned without close examination.

Fully warranted—See Page 2

ATHOL TOOLS
PREMIER OUTSIDE SPRING CALIPER
No. 200

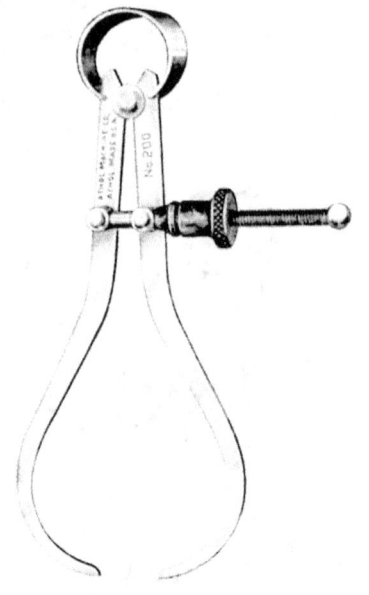

PRICES

Size	With Quick Nut	With Solid Nut
2½ in.	$0.80	$0.65
3 "	.85	.70
4 "	.90	.75
5 "	.95	.80
6 "	1.00	.85
8 "	1.15	1.00

PREMIER INSIDE SPRING CALIPER
No. 220

PRICES

Size	With Quick Nut	With Solid Nut
2½ in.	$0.80	$0.65
3 "	.85	.70
4 "	.90	.75
5 "	.95	.80
6 "	1.00	.85
8 "	1.15	1.00

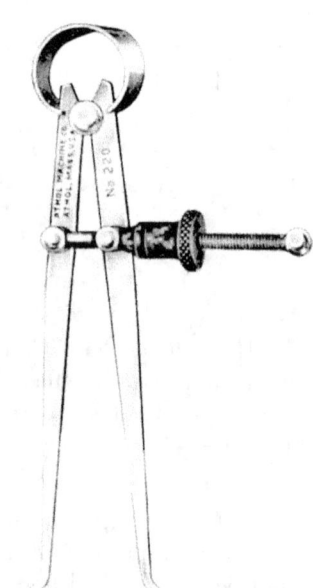

Fully warranted—See Page 2

ATHOL TOOLS
PREMIER SPRING DIVIDER
Tempered
No. 240

240
280

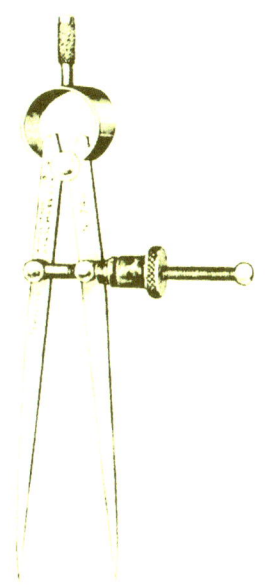

PRICES

Size	With Quick Nut	With Solid Nut
2½ in.	$0.80	$0.65
3 "	.85	.70
4 "	.90	.75
5 "	.95	.80
6 "	1.00	.85
8 "	1.25	1.10

PREMIER KEYHOLE SPRING CALIPER
No. 280
PRICES

Size	With Quick Nut	With Solid Nut
3 in.	$0.85	$0.70
4 "	.90	.75

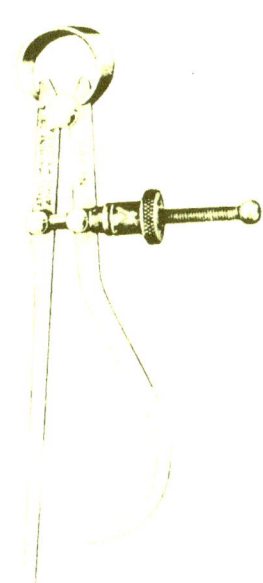

Fully warranted—See Page 2

ATHOL TOOLS

PREMIER OUTSIDE THREAD SPRING CALIPER
No. 266

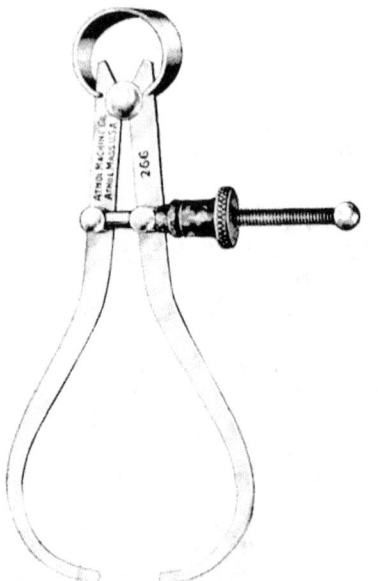

For obtaining the diameter at the bottom of an outside thread.

PRICES

Size	With Quick Nut	With Solid Nut
3 in.	$0.85	$0.70
4 "	.90	.75
5 "	.95	.80

PREMIER INSIDE THREAD SPRING CALIPER
Tempered
No. 272

For obtaining the diameter at the bottom of an inside thread.

PRICES

Size	With Quick Nut	With Solid Nut
3 in.	$0.85	$0.70
4 "	.90	.75
5 "	.95	.80

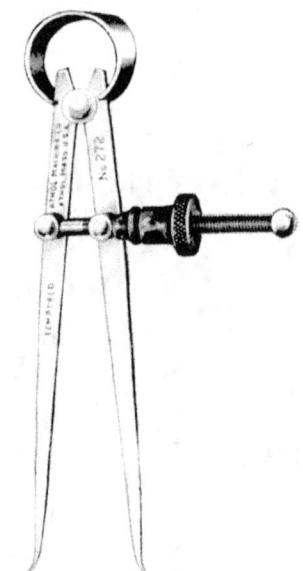

Fully warranted—See Page 2

ATHOL VISES AND TOOLS, ATHOL, MASS., U. S. A.

ATHOL TOOLS
PREMIER STRAIGHT LEG SPRING CALIPER
No. 284

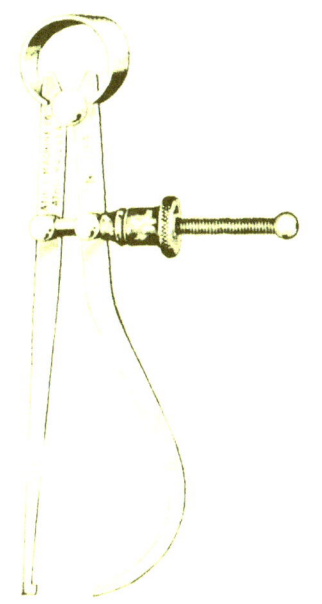

PRICES

Size	With Quick Nut	With Solid Nut
3 in.	$0.85	$0.70
4 "	.90	.75

PREMIER HERMAPHRODITE SPRING CALIPER
Tempered
No. 290

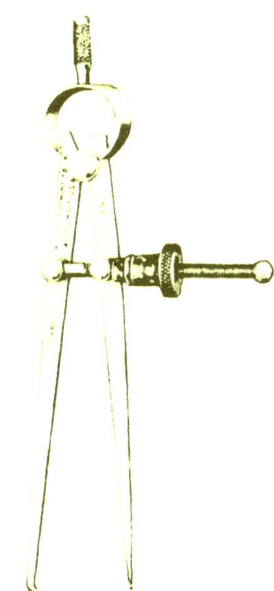

PRICES

Size	With Quick Nut	With Solid Nut
3 in.	$0.85	$0.70
4 "	.90	.75
5 "	.95	.80
6 "	1.00	.85

Fully warranted   See Page 2

ATHOL MACHINE COMPANY

300
320

ATHOL TOOLS
A. M. C. OUTSIDE SPRING CALIPER
No. 300

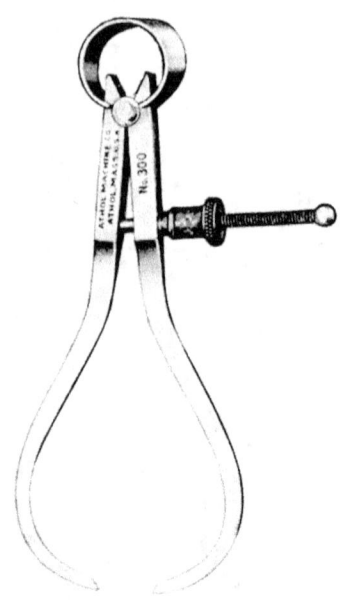

PRICES

Size	With Quick Nut	With Solid Nut
2½ in.	$1.15	$1.00
3 "	1.15	1.00
4 "	1.25	1.10
5 "	1.25	1.10
6 "	1.50	1.35
8 "	1.75	1.60

A. M. C. INSIDE SPRING CALIPER
No. 320
PRICES

Size	With Quick Nut	With Solid Nut
2½ in.	$1.15	$1.00
3 "	1.15	1.00
4 "	1.25	1.10
5 "	1.25	1.10
6 "	1.50	1.35
8 "	1.75	1.60

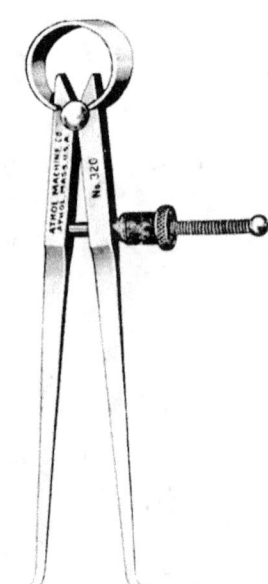

Fully warranted—See Page 2

ATHOL VISES AND TOOLS, ATHOL, MASS., U. S. A.

ATHOL TOOLS

340
360

A. M. C. SPRING DIVIDER
Tempered

No. 340

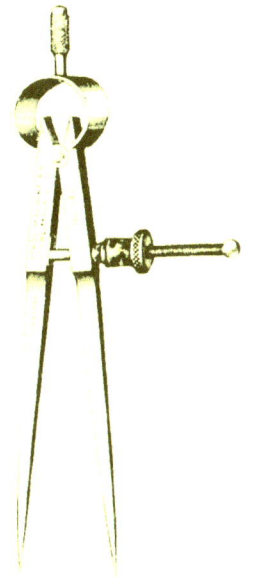

PRICES

Size	With Quick Nut	With Solid Nut
2½ in.	$1.15	$1.00
3 "	1.15	1.00
4 "	1.40	1.25
5 "	1.40	1.25
6 "	1.75	1.60
8 "	2.00	1.85

A. M. C. THREAD SPRING CALIPER

No. 360

PRICES

Size	With Quick Nut	With Solid Nut
3 in.	$1.15	$1.00
4 "	1.25	1.10
5 "	1.25	1.10

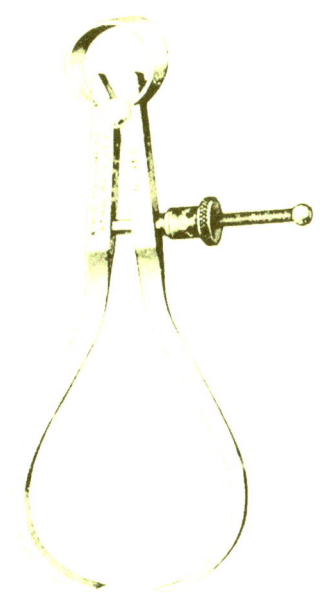

Fully warranted See Page 2

368

ATHOL TOOLS
A. M. C. KEYHOLE SPRING CALIPER
No. 368

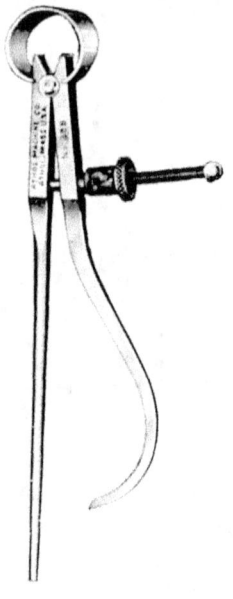

PRICES

Size	With Quick Nut	With Solid Nut
3 in.	$1.15	$1.00
4 "	1.25	1.10

Fully warranted—See Page 2

PARTS OF PREMIER CALIPERS AND DIVIDERS
PRICES

Leg	$0.25	Screw and Ball	$0.15
Spring	.25	Thumb Piece	.15
Solid Nut	.10	Fulcrum Stud	.10
Spring Nut	.25	Jam Washer	.10

PARTS OF A. M. C. CALIPERS AND DIVIDERS
PRICES

Leg	$0.35	Screw and Ball	$0.15
Spring	.25	Thumb Piece	.15
Solid Nut	.10	Fulcrum Stud	.10
Spring Nut	.25	Jam Washer	.10

ATHOL VISES AND TOOLS, ATHOL, MASS., U. S. A.

ATHOL TOOLS

530
531

FIRM JOINT INSIDE CALIPER
Tempered

No. 530

PRICES

3 in.	$0.40
4 "	.50
5 "	.55
6 "	.65
8 "	.80
10 "	.90
12 "	1.00
14 "	1.50

All our Firm Joint Calipers are made with the stud squared to fit a square hole in the leg so they can be readily adjusted to any tension desired by the operator. The friction joint is made with a fibre washer treated with our special beeswax solution. The calipers are carefully tempered.

Size given is the length of the Caliper, the capacity being about one third more.

FIRM JOINT OUTSIDE CALIPER
Tempered

No. 531

PRICES

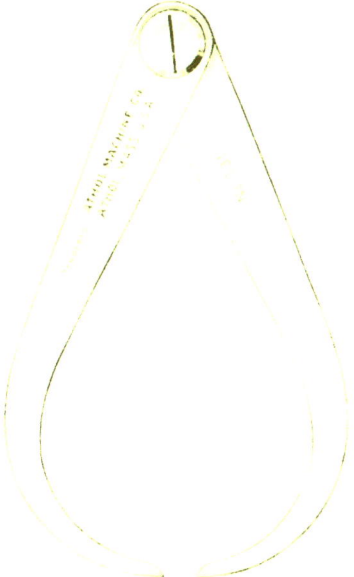

3 in.	$0.40
4 "	.50
5 "	.55
6 "	.65
8 "	.80
10 "	.90
12 "	1.00
14 "	1.50

Fully warranted   See Page 2

ATHOL MACHINE COMPANY

560
561

ATHOL TOOLS
FIRM JOINT HERMAPHRODITE CALIPER
Tempered
No. 560

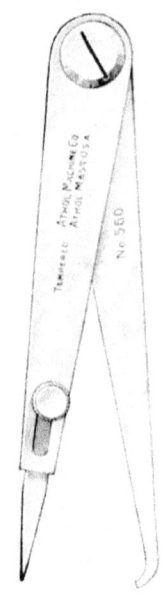

PRICES

4 in	$0.65
6 "	.80
8 "	1.00
10 "	1.20

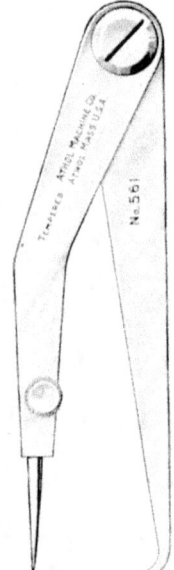

FIRM JOINT HERMAPHRODITE CALIPER
Tempered
With Bent Leg
No. 561
PRICES

4 in	$0.65
6 "	.80
8 "	1.00
10 "	1.20

Fully warranted—See Page 2

ATHOL VISES AND TOOLS, ATHOL, MASS., U. S. A.

ATHOL TOOLS
EXTENSION DIVIDER

552

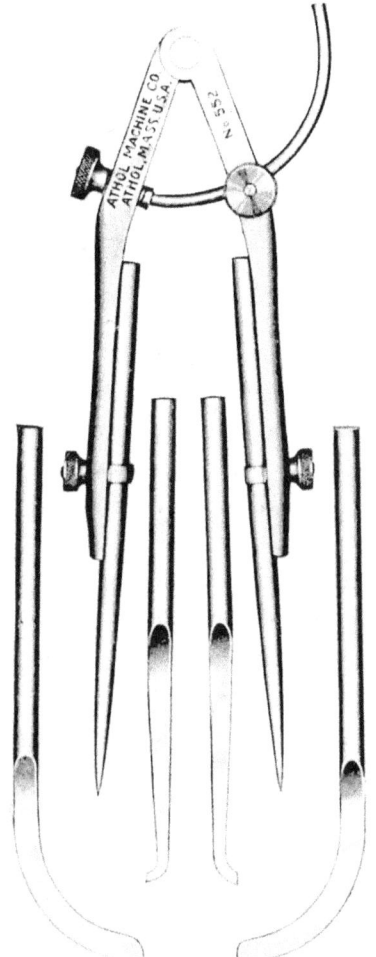

No. 552

An exceptionally well made divider with both inside and outside caliper legs any of which can be used in combination with a common pencil for carpenters use.

The movable leg is clamped to the quadrant by means of a lock bolt and loose nut which are milled on a half circle so as to give a binding effect on the quadrant without marring it. The knurled nut at the end of the quadrant is for the final fine adjustment, and tightens against a strong spring. These dividers are not to be compared with the cheap type which will only last a short time and are very unsatisfactory to use.

PRICES   CALIPER CAPACITY

Size	With Divider Legs Only	Complete	Circle Scribed	Outside Round	Outside Square	Inside
6 in.	$1.25	$2.25	28 in.	10 in.	13 in.	14 in
8 "	1.50	2.50	36 "	13 "	17 "	18 "
10 "	1.75	2.75	48 "	15 "	24 "	25 "

Sent complete unless otherwise specified.

563

ATHOL TOOLS
EXTENSION DIVIDER
No. 563

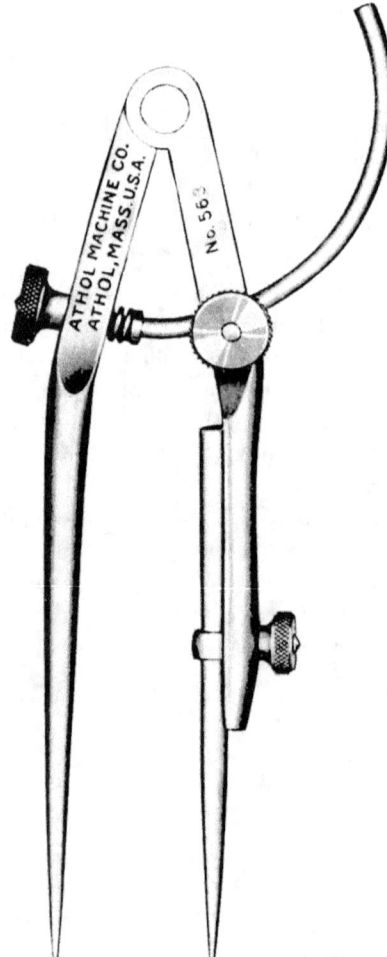

These Extension Dividers have a lock bolt and loose nut which are milled on a half circle for clamping the movable leg to the quadrant. This prevents the quadrant from becoming jammed or marred. The tool steel points are carefully tempered, one point being instantly removable so that a pencil can be inserted in its place if desired.

The knurled nut at the end of the quadrant is for the final fine adjustment, tightening against a strong spring.

In material, workmanship and all essentials, these Extension Dividers are in a class by themselves and will outwear several of the cheaper kinds.

PRICES

6 in.	$0.85
8 "	1.00
10 "	1.25

Fully warranted—See Page 2

ATHOL TOOLS

STANDARD STEEL RULE
Spring Tempered

No. 512

Specify length and style of graduation wanted.
Rules of No. 4 graduation will be sent unless otherwise ordered.

No. 1 Graduation		No. 2 Graduation	
1st corner	10, 20, 50, 100	1st corner	10, 20, 50, 100
2d "	12, 24, 48	2d "	12, 24, 48
3d "	16, 32, 64	3d "	16, 32, 64
4th "	14, 28	4th "	8

No. 4 Graduation		No. 7 Graduation	
1st corner	64	1st corner	64
2d "	32	2d "	32
3d "	16	3d "	16
4th "	8	4th "	100

PRICES

1 in.	$0.20	12 in.	$1.25
2 "	.30	18 "	2.00
3 "	.40	24 "	2.50
4 "	.50	36 "	5.00
6 "	.65	48 "	7.00
9 "	1.00		

Fully warranted—See Page 2

ATHOL TOOLS
UNIVERSAL BEVEL

No. 503

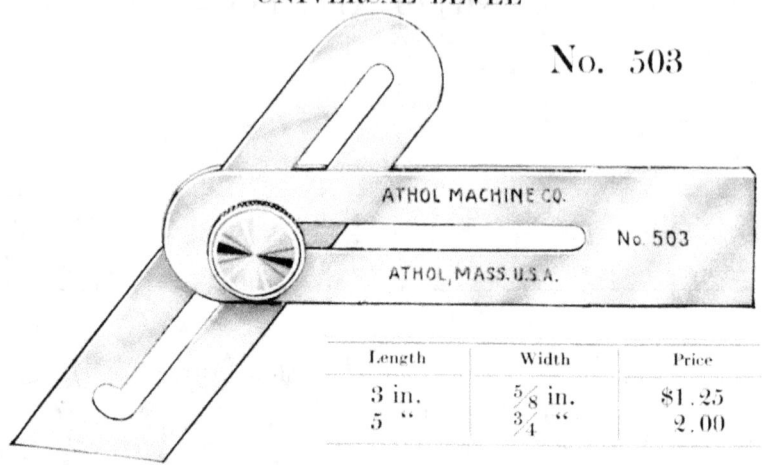

Length	Width	Price
3 in.	⅝ in.	$1.25
5 "	¾ "	2.00

UNIVERSAL BEVEL

No. 568

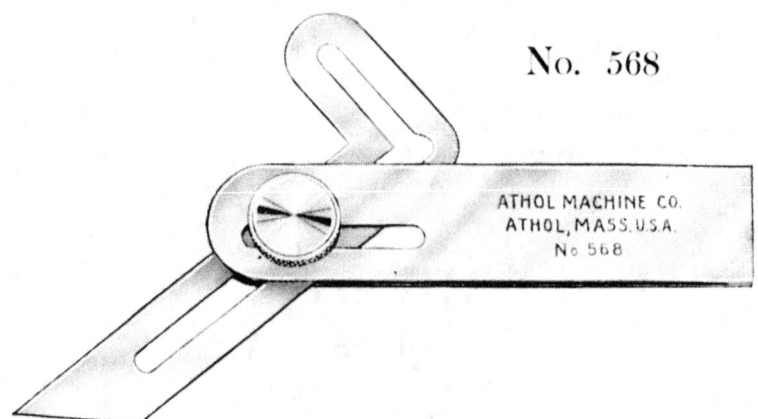

Any angle however slight, may be obtained with these Bevels. One edge of base being solid makes them convenient to use in working thin templets. They are of superior finish and workmanship and are practically indispensable in the tool-room and pattern shop.

Length	Width	Price
3 in.	⅝ in.	$1.50
5 "	¾ "	2.25

Fully warranted—See Page 2

ATHOL TOOLS
STEEL STRAIGHT EDGE
No. 513
Not Graduated

PRICES

Length	Width	Thickness	Price
12 in.	1 in.	$\frac{3}{16}$ in.	$1.20
18 "	$1\frac{1}{4}$ "	$\frac{3}{16}$ "	1.80
24 "	$1\frac{1}{2}$ "	$\frac{3}{16}$ "	2.40
36 "	2 "	$\frac{1}{4}$ "	5.00
48 "	$2\frac{1}{2}$ "	$\frac{1}{4}$ "	8.00
60 "	3 "	$\frac{1}{4}$ "	12.00
72 "	3 "	$\frac{1}{4}$ "	16.00

BEVELED STEEL STRAIGHT EDGE
No. 514
Not Graduated

The beveled edges are $\frac{1}{16}$ in. thick. Only one edge is beveled.

PRICES

Length	Width	Thickness	Price
12 in.	1 in.	$\frac{3}{16}$ in.	$1.50
18 "	$1\frac{1}{4}$ "	$\frac{3}{16}$ "	2.50
24 "	$1\frac{1}{2}$ "	$\frac{3}{16}$ "	3.50
36 "	2 "	$\frac{1}{4}$ "	6.00

Fully warranted—See Page 2

507

ATHOL TOOLS
GRADUATED DEPTH GAUGE
No. 507

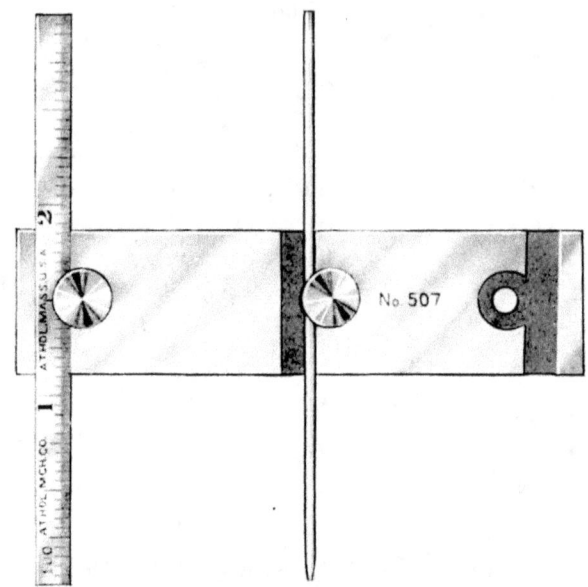

These gauges are provided with a blade, three sixteenths of an inch wide, graduated on one side in 64ths and on the other in 100ths, drawn to its seat with a screw having a thumb nut on reverse side. Both edges of the beam and the blade are accurately ground.

A wire is also sent with the gauge for use in holes too small to admit the blade and is held by a groove under the round edge of screw head.

The third slot is cut at an angle of one degree for use in die work, and for getting the draft on patterns.

PRICES

Number		Price
507 A	with 3 inch scale	$1.25
507 B	" 4 "	1.50
507 C	" 6 "	1.75

Fully warranted—See Page 2

ATHOL TOOLS
COMBINATION SQUARE
No. 500

500

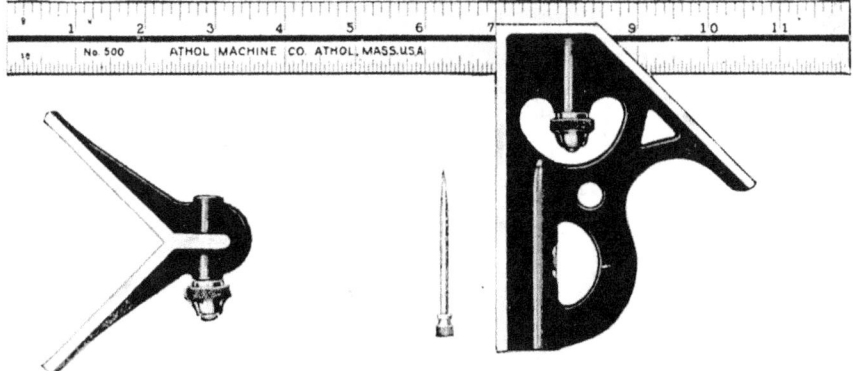

The Athol Combination Square comprises in itself a rule, square, miter, depth gauge, height gauge and level. It has a center head for centering the end of a shaft or any round piece and a scriber which is frictionally held in the head by a small brass bushing when not in use.

In order to be of any practical value a Combination Square must be accurate in all of its several parts whether they are used separately or in combination. **WE WARRANT OUR SQUARES TO BE ACCURATE.**

SET COMPLETE		WITHOUT CENTER HEAD	
Number	Price	Number	Price
500 A, 6 in	$1.50	500 B,	$1.00
500 C, 9 "	1.75	500 D,	1.25
500 E, 12 "	2.00	500 F,	1.50

A set complete comprises a Miter Head, Center Head, Blade and Scriber as shown in above cut, one blade fitting both heads.

The set complete will be sent in all cases unless otherwise specially ordered.

PRICES OF SEPARATE PARTS

Size	Blade	Miter Head	Center Head
6 in.	$0.75	$0.50	$0.50
9 "	1.00	.50	.50
12 "	1.25	.75	.50

Fully warranted—See Page 2

ATHOL TOOLS
KEY RING SCREW PITCH GAUGE
No. 566

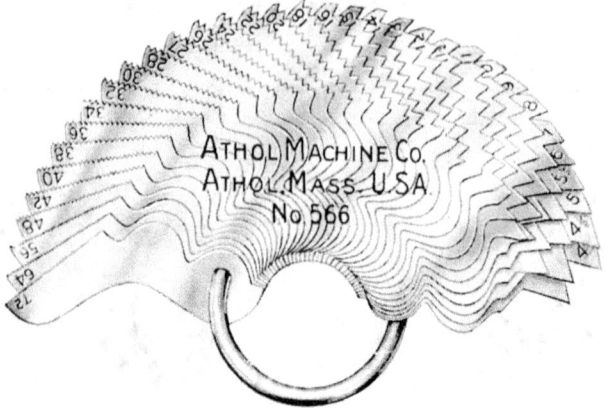

For Inside and Outside Work
A Full line of Pitches as Shown in Cut, From 4 to 72.   Price 75 cents
Furnished with Whitworth form of thread if specified

PREMIER SCREW PITCH GAUGE
With Positive Stop
No. 567

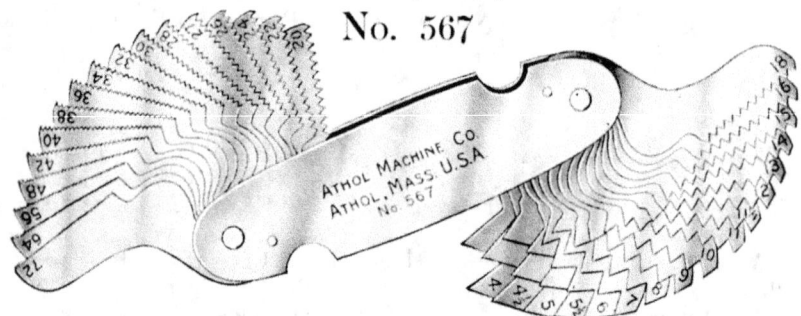

For Inside and Outside Work
A Full Line of Pitches as Shown in Cut, from 4 to 72.   Price $1.25
Furnished with Whitworth form of thread if specified

This gauge has a positive stop which will hold the blade that is being used in the handiest position. This is especially useful in determining the pitch of an inside thread as it is not necessary for the operator to get his fingers in the way and he can easily see when the threads mesh perfectly.

These tools are made absolutely accurate and are strong and dependable in every way.

Fully warranted—See Page 2

ATHOL TOOLS

509
536
537

GRADUATED CENTER GAUGE

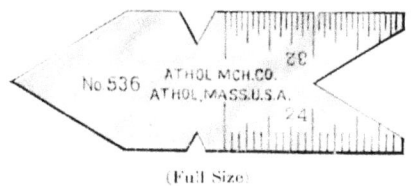

(Full Size)

Angle 60 degrees. Graduated in fourteenths, twentieths, twenty-fourths, and thirty-seconds.

PRICES

No. 536. Not tempered..$0.25
No. 537. Spring tempered...................................... .35

COMBINATION PLIER

No. 509

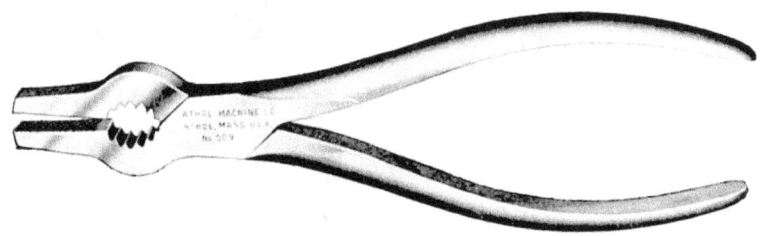

The utility of this tool will be seen at a glance. It is a combination of the common flat plier and a gas plier, and is made from the best hardened tool steel.

PRICES

5 in...$0.60
6 " .... .70
7 " .... .75

Fully warranted—See Page 2

ATHOL TOOLS
DRILL BLOCKS
No. 555

555
564

Furnished in pairs. Size each, 2 in. x 1½ in.
Price per pair..$1.00

DRILL BLOCK CLAMP
No. 564

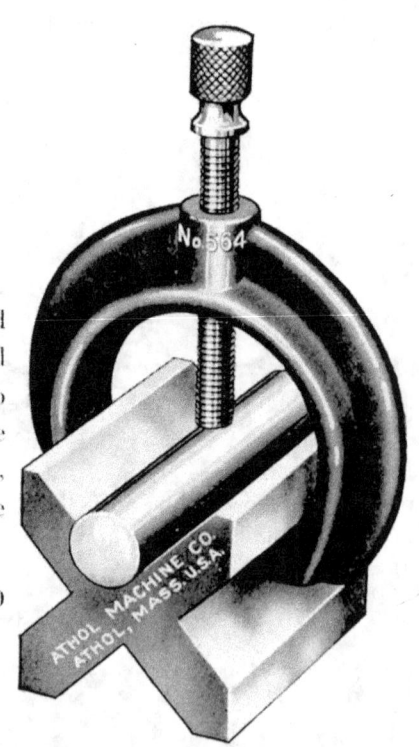

This cut shows the clamp as used in connection with No. 555 Drill Blocks. It holds the round piece up to 1⅛ in. diameter firmly in the groove for prick punching, drilling, or laying out a series of holes before and while being drilled.

Price each................$0.50

Fully warranted—See Page 2

ATHOL TOOLS

435

CARPENTERS' AND MACHINISTS' IRON LEVEL
With Double Plumb

No. 435

18 inch Level, reduced size

12 inch Level, reduced size

6 inch Level, reduced size

Base of levels grooved for cylindrical work. The groove is exactly parallel with the edge of the base.

These levels are of handsome design, accurate, and surpassed by no others on the market.

The 4 in. has level vial only; the other sizes have double plumbs.

Length	Price
4 inch, each	$1.35
6 " "	1.50
9 " "	1.65
12 " "	1.75
18 " "	2.00
24 " "	2.25

With adjustable vial in level, any size except 4 inch, extra, $0.50 each.

Fully warranted—See Page 2

ATHOL TOOLS
IRON POCKET LEVEL
No. 436

Warranted accurate

PRICES

2½ in.	$0.25
3½ "	.30

GROVED LEVEL
No. 438

Made with a deep groove running the entire length so it can be used on piping, shafting, or any cylindrical work.

PRICES

6 in., $1.50   9 in., $1.65   12 in., $1.75

Fully warranted—See Page 2

ATHOL TOOLS

439
442

ENGINEERS' AND PLUMBERS' LEVEL

No. 439

This level is grooved on the bottom the whole length, which any one who has occasion to level up shafting, piping, etc., will see the advantage of, as it enables the user to place the level in line with the shaft or pipe as readily as on a flat surface. These levels are so made that they can be used on a flat surface the same as ordinary levels. This level has a graduated plate on one end that can be adjusted to give the exact pitch of pipes, etc.

PRICES

6 in....................$2.00   12 in....................$2.25

NICKEL PLATED POCKET LEVEL

No. 442

PRICES

$2\frac{1}{2}$ in....................$0.40 $3\frac{1}{2}$ in....................$0.50

Fully warranted—See Page 2

557

ATHOL TOOLS
TOOLMAKERS PARALLEL CLAMP
No. 557

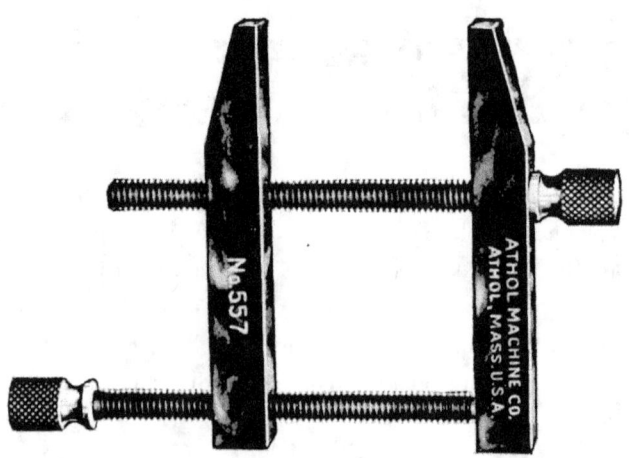

These Clamps are made of steel, hardened in cyanide and left with a beautiful mottled finish. They are almost indispensable to Machinists and Toolmakers for holding small work together when drilling, tapping or fitting.

PRICES

Size	Jaws Open	Price
1½ in.	1 in.	$0.50
2 "	1¼ "	.65
2½ "	1¾ "	.75
3 "	2¼ "	.85

Prices are for single clamp.

Fully warranted—See Page 2

ATHOL TOOLS
MACHINISTS' CLAMP
No. 544

544

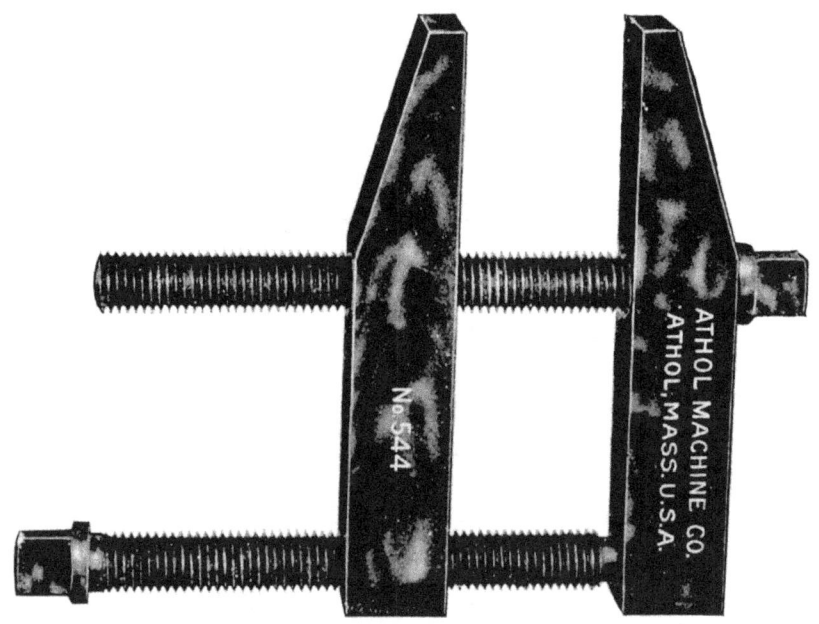

Strong enough for rough usage.

Made from steel, case-hardened and ground true.   Hardened screws.

PRICES

Size	Jaws Open	Price
2 in.	1½ in.	$0.75
3 "	2½ "	1.00
4 "	3 "	1.25
5 "	3½ "	1.50
6 "	5¼ "	1.75

Prices are for single clamp.

Fully warranted—See Page 2

540

ATHOL TOOLS
THE BOSS HAND VISE
No. 540

This Vise (except handle) is hardened throughout and finely finished, with polished jaws.

Number	Width Jaws	Jaws Open	Weight	Price
540 A	1¼ in.	¾ in.	1-2 lb.	$0.75
540 B	1½ in.	1 in.	3-4 lb.	1.00

Fully warranted—See Page 2.

ATHOL TOOLS
STANDARD HAND VISE
No. 549

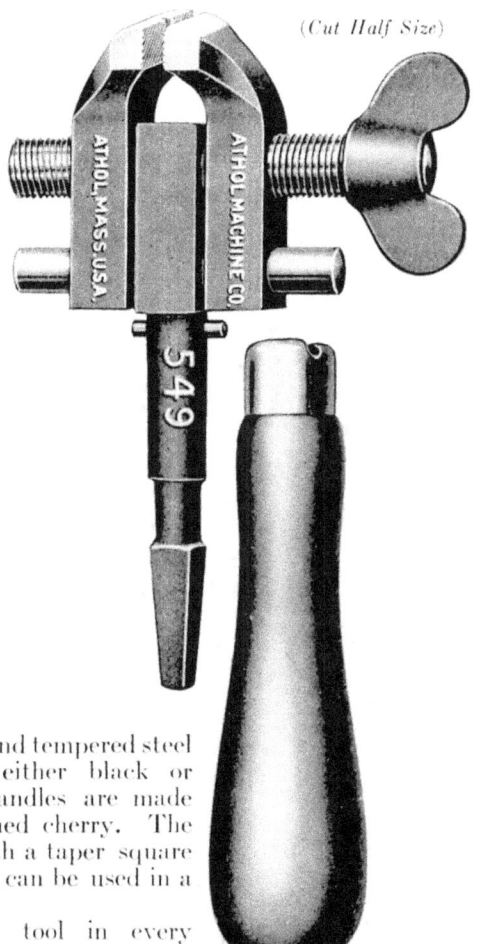

(Cut Half Size)

Drop forged and tempered steel jaws, finished either black or bright. The handles are made of highly polished cherry. The vise is made with a taper square shank so that it can be used in a bit brace.

A first-class tool in every respect.

	Width Jaws	Jaws Open	Weight	Price
No. 549 A.	1¼ in. Black	1¼ in.	14 oz.	$1.25
No. 549 B.	1¼ in. Bright	1¼ in.	14 oz.	1.50
No. 549 C.	1½ in. Black	1½ in.	18 oz.	1.50
No. 549 D.	1½ in. Bright	1½ in.	18 oz.	1.75

Fully warranted—See Page 2.

RAPID TRANSIT WRENCH No. 541

541

For use on Motor Boats, Automobiles and by Mechanics generally.

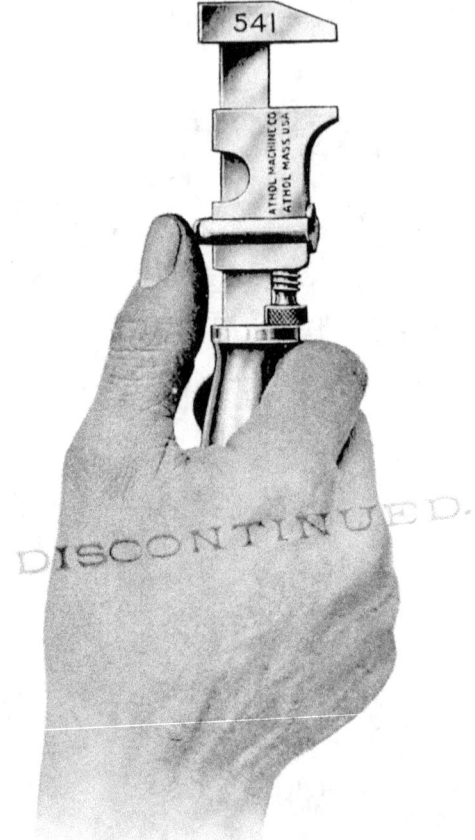

METHOD OF OPERATING WRENCH

The method of operating is so clearly shown in the cut that a description seems almost needless. A slight pressure of the thumb disengages the nut from the screw, permitting the jaw to be moved rapidly the full length of the bar, and as soon as the pressure is removed the nut instantly resumes its place, and the screw can be used to tighten the grip if necessary. We believe it to be the best wrench on the market, and one that every workman will appreciate.

PRICES

No. 541 A.	6 in. Black	$0.75
No. 541 B.	6 in. Bright	1.00

ATHOL TOOLS
LEVELING INSTRUMENT
No. 441

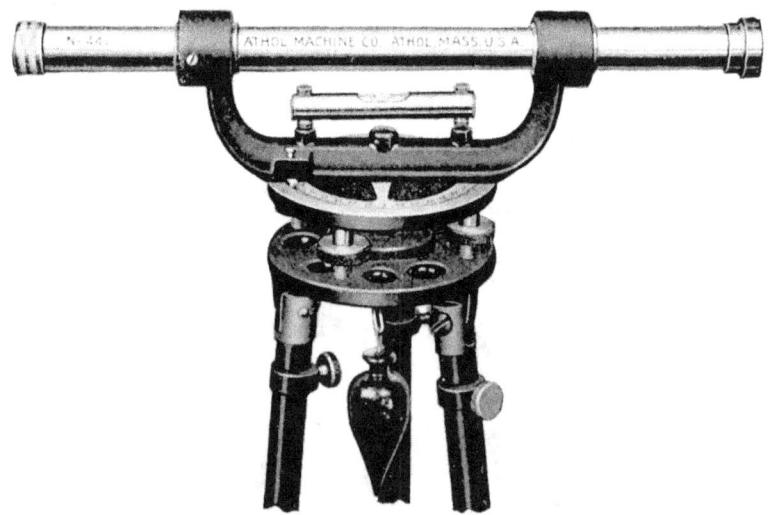

Warranted to be true in every respect.

The best, the cheapest, and most durable in the market for the money.

It is adapted for the use of architects, carpenters, builders, stone masons, and others, for leveling, getting angles, etc.

It is made of iron, japanned, except the sight tube, which is of brass, nickel plated. It weighs, when packed in box for shipment, $13\frac{3}{4}$ pounds. Directions sent with instrument.

PRICES

No. 441 A.	Japanned, nickeled tube	$12.50
No. 441 B.	Japanned, nickeled tube, with ground vial in level	14.00

Fully warranted—See Page 2

440

ATHOL TOOLS
TRANSIT
No. 440

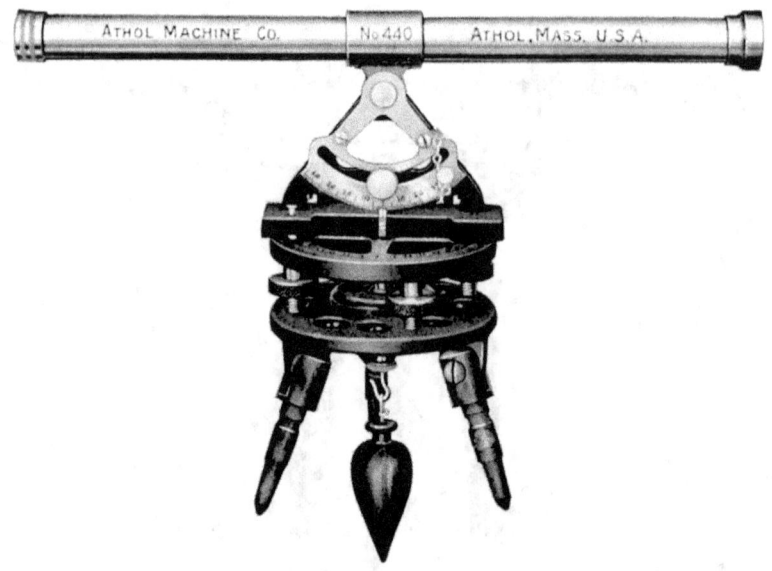

This instrument consists of a tripod, to the head of which is connected an upper plate carrying a graduated arc and a level with plain sight tube.

It is designed for architects, carpenters, and contractors, to lay out building sites and determine the levels; for masons and millwrights in the construction of foundations and the setting of water wheels; building of dams and raceways. The farmer will find it convenient to ascertain the amount of fall for the location of drains, or to find the height of springs; and, when the bearing of lines is not required, the surveyor will find this superior to the ordinary needle compass, for angles may be taken where, from local attraction, it would not be possible to set them off with the needle.

It will be especially appreciated by all who need a level and some instrument for the taking of angles, but do not care to pay the price usually charged for a surveyor's or engineer's transit.

Fully warranted—See Page 2

ATHOL TOOLS 440
TRANSIT
No. 440—Continued

The instrument is composed of iron and brass, and consists of a tripod, to the head of which is connected by a ball-and-socket joint an upper plate, which can be leveled by the leveling screws.

This plate is recessed to contain a graduated arc for taking angles. On this plate rests a triangular frame to which are attached a level, a graduated arc for taking vertical angles, and a sight tube. The plain sight tube has no lenses, is brass, twelve inches long; in one end is a small eye aperture, in the other the usual cross wires.

The telescope has cross lines, is adjustable to distances, and is same size and length as plain sight tube.

With short legs, as shown in the cut, the instrument is eight inches high. With long extension legs, which fasten on over the short, the height can be from two feet eight inches to four feet eight inches. The sight tube, level case, and graduated arcs are nickel plated, the other parts are japanned.

The advantages of this transit are as follows: The head is held to the tripod with a bolt and nut, so as to make it stationary at any given point; the graduated arc can be clamped to the base-plate by throwing a small cam arrangement.

All points taken into consideration, this transit is one of the best of its kind in the market. It is adapted to almost all kinds of work, is made of the best of materials, and finished and adjusted by skilled workmen. It is warranted perfect and accurate in every respect.

When packed and ready for shipment it weighs about 15 pounds.

Directions for setting up and using are inclosed with each transit, and will be mailed on request to any one interested.

No. 440 F will be sent when style is not specified.

PRICES

No. 440 A	With plain sight tube and short legs	$15.00
No. 440 B	With plain sight tube and long legs	17.00
No. 440 C	With plain sight tube, short legs, and ground level vial	16.50
No. 440 D	With plain sight tube, long legs, and ground level vial	18.50
No. 440 E	With telescope, short legs, and ground level vial	31.00
No. 440 F	With telescope, long legs, and ground level vial	33.00

Target to go on common ten-foot pole, extra $1.50.

Fully warranted—See Page 2

ATHOL MACHINE COMPANY

400

DOMESTIC PRESS No. 400

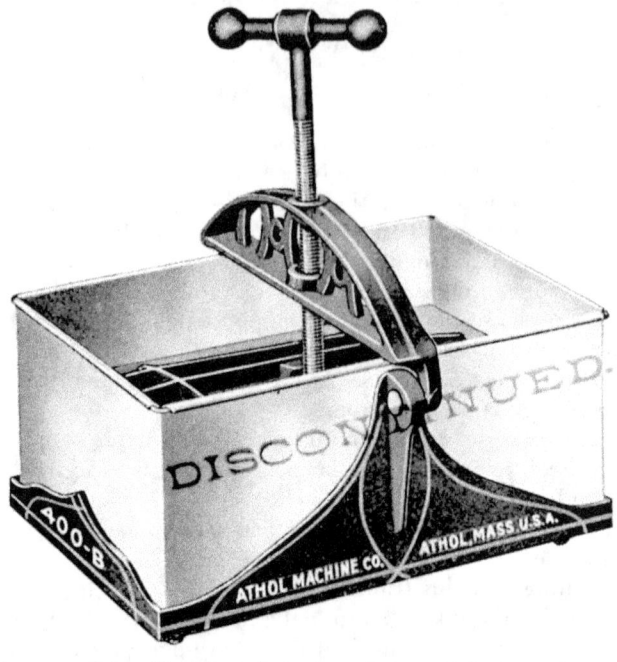

For the use of families, hotels and restaurants in pressing corned beef, boiled mutton, tongue, boned turkey, headcheese and other meats, and in extracting the juice from fruit and berries, for making domestic wines, grape and current jellies, etc.; also for pressing lard, cottage cheese, squash, turnip and other vegetables.

Corned beef, tongue, boiled chicken and all meats designed to be eaten cold, are greatly improved by being pressed, as a single trial will demonstrate. The meat should be placed in the press while hot, the fat and lean in layers, and be allowed to remain under pressure until thoroughly cooled. Meats thus treated retain their juices, have a more delicate flavor, and, when wanted for the table, can be served in a style otherwise quite impossible.

PRICES

No. 400 A.	Size, 6 x 9 and 4 in. deep	$2.50
No. 400 B.	Size, 8 x 12 and 5 in. deep	3.50
No. 400 C.	Size, 10 x 14 and 6 in. deep	4.50

PRICES OF PARTS

	No. 400 A	No. 400 B	No. 400 C
Yoke	$0.33	$0.42	$0.50
Screw	.25	.35	.40
Follower	.40	.60	.80
Perforated Tin	.25	.33	.40
Base and Rim	1.50	2.00	2.50

ATHOL VISES AND TOOLS, ATHOL, MASS., U. S. A

WRIGHT'S ANIMAL TETHER
No. 415

415

The cut shows the advantages of this invention, which is designed to obviate the danger of horses and other animals becoming entangled in the rope with which they are fastened. It consists of a pole about ten feet in length, connected with an upright bar, upon which it turns in any direction. The animal is fastened to the end of this pole by a rope, which is kept taut above his head by means of a spring at the base of the pole; this keeps the pole high in the air, until in reaching for the feed the animal pulls it down, thus at all times keeping the rope from under his feet.

PRICES OF PARTS

Spring	$0.75
Bar Holder	.30
Pole Holder	.25
Rivet	.05
Bar	.75
Rope	.25
Upper Collar	.25
Lower Collar	.15
Pole	.25
Thumb Screw	.15

Price, $3.00

ATHOL   MACHINE   COMPANY

INDEX

VISES

Pages 6 to 47

	Pages
Amateur	39
Carpenters' and Coachmakers'	34 and 35
Combination Pipe	36 and 37
Display Stands	4 to 13
Farmers'	39
Hand	80 and 81
Machinists':	
Simpson, Quick Acting	30 to 35
Six Hundred Line	22 to 25
Standard	26 to 28
Starrett Patent Improved	14 to 21
Oval Slide	40
Pipe Grips	38
Taper Attachments	29

MACHINISTS' VISES

Indexed by Type

	Pages
Stationary Base, Stationary Jaw	16–26–32
Stationary Base, Swivel Jaw	20–24
Swivel Base, Stationary Jaw	17–23–27–31–33
Swivel Base, Swivel Jaw	21–25
Clamp Base	15–28–31–39

GRINDSTONE FRAMES, GRINDERS

	Pages
Bench Grinders	46 and 47
Countershaft	48
Grindstone Frames	41 to 44
Grindstone Truer	45

ATHOL VISES AND TOOLS, ATHOL, MASS., U. S. A.

INDEX

TOOLS

	Pages
Attachments, Adjustable Taper	29
Bevels, Universal	68
Calipers and Dividers	55 to 66
Clamps, Drill Block	74
Clamps, Machinists	79
Clamps, Toolmakers	78
Dividers and Calipers	55 to 66
Drill Blocks	74
Gauges, Center	73
Gauges, Depth	70
Gauges, Screw Pitch	72
Leveling Instrument	83
Levels	75 to 77
Pliers, Combination	73
Rules	67
Straight Edges	69
Squares, Combination	71
Transit	84 and 85
Wrench	82

MISCELLANEOUS

Press (Meat and Vegetable)	86
Tether (Animal)	87

NUMERICAL INDEX

(Continued)

Catalogue Number	Page	Catalogue Number	Page	Catalogue Number	Page
0	31	60	39	93	26
1	31	62	39	94	26
2	31	63	40	95	26
3	28	64	40	96	26
4	28	65	40	97	26
5	28	66	40		
6	28	67	40		
				144	37
10	31	69	39	145	36
11	33	70	39	146	37
12	33	71	39	147	36
13	33	72	39	148	37
14	33			149	36
15	33			150	38
16	33	77	27		
		78	27		
		79	27		
27	32	80	27	154	41
28	32	81	27	155	42
29	32	82	27	156	43
30	32	83	27	157	44
31	32			158	46
32	32			159	47
33	32	87	26	160	48
		88	26	161	45
40	34	89	26		
41	34	90	26		
42	35	91	26	192	29
43	35	92	26	193	29

NUMERICAL INDEX

(Continued)

Catalogue Number	Page
200	56
220	56
240	57
266	58
272	58
280	57
284	59
290	59
300	60
320	60
340	61
360	61
368	62
435	75
436	76
438	76
439	77
440	84
441	83

Catalogue Number	Page
442	77
500	71
503	68
507	70
509	73
512	67
513	69
514	69
530	63
531	63
536	73
537	73
540	80
541	82
544	79
549	81
552	65

Catalogue Number	Page
555	74
557	78
560	64
561	64
563	66
564	74
566	72
567	72
568	68
624	25
625	24
626	25
627	24
628	25
629	24
630	25
631	24
632	25
633	24
634	25
635	24
636	25
637	24

NUMERICAL INDEX
(Concluded)

Catalogue Number	Page	Catalogue Number	Page	Catalogue Number	Page
677	23	708	17	727	20
678	23	709	16	728	21
679	23	710	17	729	20
680	23	711	16	730	21
681	23	712	17	731	20
682	23	713	16	732	21
683	23	714	17	733	20
684	23	715	16	734	21
685	23	716	17	735	20
686	23	717	16	736	21
687	23	718	17	737	20
701	15	719	16		
703	15	720	17		
704	17	721	16	A	6
705	16	724	21	B	8
706	17	725	20	C	10
707	16	726	21	D	12

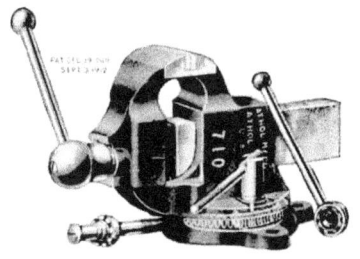

STRONG WHERE STRENGTH IS NEEDED

We believe the GOLDEN RULE can be followed even where vise predominates.

www.ingramcontent.com/pod-product-compliance
Lightning Source LLC
Chambersburg PA
CBHW071219070526
44584CB00019B/3080